# STECK-VAUGHN
# Spelling

John R. Pescosolido, Ph.D.
Professor Emeritus
Central Connecticut State University
New Britain, Connecticut

Consultants

Felice M. Rockoff
Reading Teacher
New York City Public Schools
New York, New York

Theodore J. Thibodeau
Assistant Superintendent
Attleboro Public Schools
Attleboro, Massachusetts

Anna L. Ulrich
Adjunct Professor
College of Santa Fe
Albuquerque, New Mexico

Anita Uphaus
Coordinator of Early Childhood Programs
Austin Independent School District
Austin, Texas

STECK-VAUGHN
COMPANY
ELEMENTARY • SECONDARY • ADULT • LIBRARY

# Acknowledgments

**Executive Editor**: Diane Sharpe
**Project Editor:** Amanda Johnson
**Design Manager:** Richard Balsam
**Designers:** Jim Cauthron
Danielle Szabo

**Product Development:** Cottage Communications
**Typesetting:** Publishers' Design and Production Services, Inc.

**Writers:** Patricia Crittenden (pp. 102, 108, 120); Linda Ekblad (pp. 88, 166, 190); Carol Ellis (pp. 30, 62, 114, 134, 152, 158); Bernice Golden (p. 18); Roberta Green (pp. 94, 140); Bobbi Katz (p. 184); Phyllis Keaton (pp. 12, 24, 56, 76); Colleen Normandin (p. 70); Alice Pernick (p. 44); Julia Remine Piggin (pp. 82, 172); Stuart Podhaizer (etymologies); Leslie Purificación (pp. 146, 178); Carole Ridolfino (p. 126); Joan Rosenblatt (p. 38); Lorraine Sotiriou (p. 50); Doreen Nation Ziobro (p. 6)

**Artists:** Duane Bibby, Paige Billin-Frye, Maxie Chambliss, Brian Cody, Eulala Conner, Diane Dawson, Betsy Day, Arlene Dubanevich, Julie Durrell, Jon Friedman, John Gamache, Jon Goodell, Carol Grosvenor, Konrad Hack, Meryl Henderson, Ruth Hoffman, True Kelley, Elizabeth Koda-Callan, Mike Krone, Dora Leder, Tom Leonard, Susan Lexa, Jan Pyk, Marcy Ramsey, Jerry Smath, Arthur Thompson, Pat Traub, John Wallner, Kathy Wilburn, Lane Yerkes

Grateful acknowledgment is made to the following for the use of copyrighted materials. Every effort has been made to obtain permission to use previously published material. Any errors or omissions are unintentional.

Pronunciation key and diacritical marks in the Spelling Dictionary copyright © 1994 by Houghton Mifflin Company. Reprinted by permission from *THE AMERICAN HERITAGE STUDENT DICTIONARY.*

**ISBN 0-8114-9272-9**

# Contents

# Lesson 1    Words with /ă/

**Listen for /ă/ as you say each word.**

ask

matter

black

add

match

Saturday

class

apple

subtract

thank

catch

January

after

hammer

half

laugh

1. Write four words that begin with the vowel sound /ă/.

_____    _____

_____    _____

2. Write two words that end with the sound /f/.

_____    _____

3. Write three words that end with the sound /k/.

_____    _____

_____

4. Write two words that end with the last four letters of <u>hatch</u>.

_____    _____

5. Write two words that are always spelled with a capital letter.

_____    _____

6. Write the word that ends with the letter <u>t</u>.

_____

7. Write five words that have double consonants.

dd _____    pp _____

ss _____    tt _____

mm _____

# Checkpoint

Write a spelling word for each clue.
Then use the Checkpoint Study Plan on page 224.

1. A tool you use to hit a nail is a ____.

2. When someone tells a funny joke, you ____.

3. The color of coal is ____.

4. If there's a problem, ask, "What's the ____?"

5. To get the sum, you ____.

6. When a ball is thrown to you, you ____.

7. A round, red fruit is an ____.

8. To take away from is to ____.

9. To question is to ____.

10. Students and a teacher are a ____.

11. You ____ someone for a gift.

12. It's not the whole thing, but ____.

13. The opposite of before is ____.

14. The first month of the year is ____.

15. To make a fire use a ____.

16. This mystery word is very old. And it looked different long ago. It comes from two Old English words. The first is *Saeter*. The second is *daeg*. *Saeter* was the name of the Roman god Saturn. *Daeg* meant day. Say these two words together to give yourself a clue to the mystery word. ____

5

# Alphabetical Order

When words are in <u>a</u>-<u>b</u>-<u>c</u> order, they are in alphabetical order. This group of words is in alphabetical order:

*bend    friend    horse*

This group of words is not in alphabetical order:

*egg    animal    chicken*

⭐ Put the following groups of words in alphabetical order.

1. add    January    hammer

_____

_____

_____

2. matter    half    class

_____

_____

_____

3. thank    ask    Saturday

_____

_____

_____

4. black    subtract    catch

_____

_____

_____

5. match    laugh    apple

_____

_____

_____

# WORDS AT WORK

## Challenge Yourself

**plaid    agony    clank    fragile**

Use your Spelling Dictionary to answer these questions. Then write sentences showing that you understand the meaning of each Challenge Word.

1. Does a <u>plaid</u> shirt have one color or many colors?

2. Would you be in <u>agony</u> if you hit your thumb with a hammer?

3. Does an old iron gate <u>clank</u> when it swings shut?

4. Would you want to play in a <u>fragile</u> tree house?

## Write to the Point

Robbie felt silly when he remembered it was Saturday. Have you ever done something silly? Write a paragraph about that silly thing. Tell what happened. Use spelling words from this lesson in your paragraph.

**Challenge** Use one or more of the Challenge Words in your paragraph.

## Proofreading

Use the marks to show the errors in the sentences below. Write the four misspelled words correctly in the blanks.

| | |
|---|---|
| ⬭ | word is misspelled |
| ⊙ | period is missing |
| ≡ | letter should be capitalized |

1. I run to cach the school bus.

2. al starts to laff when I get on

3. "What's the mater?" I ask him.

4. "Your socks don't mache!" he says

1. _____

2. _____

3. _____

4. _____

9

# Lesson 2    Words with /ā/

**Listen for /ā/ as you say each word.**

ate

late

safe

page

face

save

place

came

change

gray

away

pay

May

break

great

April

1. Which two words begin with capital letters?

_____    _____

2. Write two words that have the letters <u>ate</u>.

_____    _____

3. Write four words that end with the last two letters of <u>say</u>.

_____    _____

_____    _____

4. Write the word that begins with /k/.

_____

5. Write two words in which you hear /j/ but do not see the letter <u>j</u>.

_____    _____

6. Which two words begin with the letter <u>s</u>?

_____    _____

7. Write two words in which you hear /s/ at the end but do not see the letter <u>s</u>.

_____    _____

8. In which two words is /ā/ spelled with the letters <u>ea</u>? _____

9. Which two words have two syllables?

10

# Checkpoint

Write a spelling word for each clue.
Then use the Checkpoint Study Plan on page 224.

1. Something that's terrific or wonderful is ____.

2. When you mix black and white, you get ____.

3. To rescue from danger is to ____.

4. If it's not near, it's far ____.

5. The fifth month of the year is ____.

6. Your eyes, nose, and mouth are on your ____.

7. If you don't stay the same, you ____.

8. Today you eat, yesterday you ____.

9. A certain spot is a ____.

10. To crack is to ____.

11. If it's not early, it's ____.

12. A tree has a leaf, a book has a ____.

13. The past tense of come is ____.

14. If it's not free, you must ____.

15. Where there's no danger, it is ____.

16. English has borrowed words from many other languages. The mystery word comes from the Latin word *aperilis*. *Aperilis* means "open." It names the time of year when flowers begin to open. Can you guess the word? ____

11

Use each word once to complete these pages.

# The Wheels

"Look!" laughed Anna as she _____ her breakfast. She pointed outside at a man in a _____ suit. The man's face was very red.

The man sat on a saddle. But the saddle was not on a horse. It was between two carriage wheels placed one in front of the other. And the man was trying to run while sitting down. He used handles to steer _____ from other people.

"It's the Baron," Anna's father said. "He'll _____ a leg on that strange gadget. I wouldn't _____ a penny for one of those!"

Anna's father was wrong. Baron von Drais's "strange gadget" was the first real bicycle. It was called the <u>draisine</u>. It was invented in 1816 to help people _____ time getting places. But the <u>draisine</u> didn't pass the test. It was too slow to help people who were _____.

Many changes took _____. In 1839, a wonderful _____ was made. A man put pedals on his bicycle. Now a person could ride a bicycle with both feet off the ground. Macmillan's new bicycle turned a _____ in the bicycle history book.

In 1866, Pierre Lallement invented a new bicycle. It was called the boneshaker. That was a good name for it. If you were not careful, it would shake you up. You could fall flat on your _____! It was dangerous.

In 1869, the <u>Phantom</u> made its appearance. It was made of iron, not wood. It _____ with rubber tires. Best of all, it was _____. The days of the boneshaker had ended. Bicycles were becoming like the bikes we ride today. The Baron's "strange gadget" turned out to be a _____ idea.

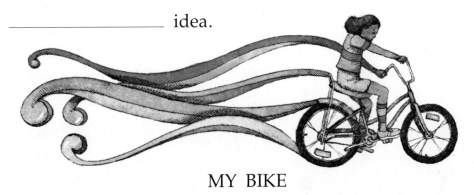

MY BIKE

The best month for riding my bike is _____,
Because in _____ it rains every day!

13

ate
late
safe
page
face
save
place
came
change
gray
away
pay
May
break
great
April

# Capitals and Periods

Begin the first word of a sentence with a capital letter.

<u>M</u>y sister collects postage stamps.

Put a period (.) at the end of a sentence that tells or explains something. Most sentences end with a period.

The first postage stamp was made in England.

★ Write the story below using these spelling words. Correct capital letters and put periods where they belong.

**May    face    save    place    late**
**safe    page    gray    away**

heather likes to ___ stamps  she keeps them ___ in

a dry ___  she must keep them ___ from her new ___  puppy

last ___, Heather went to her stamp club  she went in the

morning  a ___ fell out of her stamp book before she left  she

looked all over the place for the page when she got home

then she looked at her puppy  the hair on his ___ looked

stuck together  guess who had a ___ breakfast

# WORDS AT WORK

## Challenge Yourself

cable    debate    dismay    labor

What do you think each underlined Challenge Word means? Check your Spelling Dictionary to see if you are right. Then write sentences showing that you understand the meaning of each Challenge Word.

1. A cable holds up the bridge.

2. She will debate whether to buy a new bike or fix her old one.

3. I felt dismay when I saw the flat tire on my bike.

4. Riding up the steep hill required a great deal of labor.

## Write to the Point

People learn about new products by reading ads. Write an ad for one of the early bikes. Use words that will make people want to buy a bike. Describe the fun they can have riding one. Use spelling words from this lesson in your ad.

**Challenge** Use one or more of the Challenge Words in your ad.

## Proofreading

Use the marks to show the errors in the sentences below. Write the four misspelled words correctly in the blanks.

| | |
|---|---|
| ⬭ | word is misspelled |
| ⊙ | period is missing |
| ≡ | letter should be capitalized |

1. It's a graet day for a bike ride.

2. the gra clouds have blown away.

3. bike helmets will keep us saif.

4. I helped to paye for my new bike

1. _____

2. _____

3. _____

4. _____

15

# Lesson 3 Words with /ā/

**Listen for /ā/ as you say each word.**

paint

rain

aid

wait

train

aim

sail

afraid

paper

danger

fable

able

table

weigh

eight

they

1. Write four words that end with /l/.

   _____  _____

2. Write two words that end with the letters <u>er</u>.

   _____

3. Write two words in which /ā/ is spelled <u>ei</u>.

   _____

4. Which two words end with the last three letters of <u>pain</u>?

   _____

5. Write three words that begin with the sound /ā/.

   _____  _____

6. Which two words begin with the letter <u>w</u>?

   _____  _____

7. Write the word that begins with the letters <u>th</u>.

   _____

8. Which word begins and ends like <u>point</u>?

   _____

9. Which two words end with the letter <u>d</u>?

   _____  _____

# Checkpoint

Write a spelling word for each clue.
Then use the Checkpoint Study Plan on page 224.

1. A story that teaches a lesson is a ___ .

2. Something that falls but doesn't get hurt is ___ .

3. If you could get hurt, you're in ___ .

4. In a car you drive, on a boat you ___ .

5. Another word for scared is ___ .

6. When you eat dinner, you sit at the ___ .

7. To help someone is to give him ___ .

8. A group of connected railroad cars is a ___ .

9. You count five, six, seven, ___ .

10. A word that means stop is ___ .

11. If you can do something, you are ___ .

12. To point at something is to ___ .

13. To find out how many pounds, you ___ .

14. You write us and we, them and ___ .

15. Coloring used to make pictures is ___ .

16. Long ago in England, people wrote on tree
bark. In China, people wrote on silk and
bamboo. Around the Mediterranean Sea, people
wrote on something called *papyrus*. *Papyrus* was
made of dried grass. Today most people use
another material to write on. It is made of
finely cut wood. The name of this material
comes from the word *papyrus*. This is the
mystery word. Can you guess it? ___

Use each word once to complete this story.

# The Happy Village

It's easy to make your own little village. You can make it with paper and paste.

To begin, spread pieces of paper on top of a desk or _____. Then tear more pieces of _____ into strips. Then mix one cup of flour with enough water to make paste. Use the tops of seven or _____ milk cartons for the buildings.

Wet a few strips of paper with water. Then coat the strips of paper with the paste. Don't be _____ to use a lot of paste. Wind the paper around a milk carton. You will be _____ to make any building shape by adding more paper.

Have a wet towel to _____ you when your hands become sticky. You should _____ to work for an hour. Then stop and _____ for the piece to dry before you paint.

Later, get a brush and _____

the building.

To make the ground, use the paste over

crumpled newspaper. When dry, paint it green.

Then paint a lake. Make a boat to _____

in the lake.

Your village needs a train station. Make a

_____ using old matchboxes for the cars.

Make the train tracks out of toothpicks. Buttons

work well for train wheels because _____

are round and small.

You can add mountains and bridges. You can

even add a sign to tell of _____,

like "Falling Rocks" or "Bridge Out."

What is missing? People! There is a saying from

an old _____ ."A village without people

is like a fruit without taste." Make tiny clay people.

If they don't _____ too much you might

put them in your boat. They won't get wet. In

your village, it will never _____.

*paint*
*rain*
*aid*
*wait*
*train*
*aim*
*sail*
*afraid*
*paper*
*danger*
*fable*
*able*
*table*
*weigh*
*eight*
*they*

Falling
Rocks

19

# Compound Words

When two words are used together as one word, the new word is a compound word.

*base* + *ball* makes the compound word *baseball*
*chop* + *sticks* makes the compound word *chopsticks*

★ Match a word in List A with a word in List B and write a compound word.

| List A | List B | Compound Words |
| --- | --- | --- |
| 1. sail | weight | |
| 2. paint | top | |
| 3. paper | boat | |
| 4. rain | box | |
| 5. table | bow | |
| 6. mail | brush | |

★ Then write a sentence using each compound word you just made. Circle the compound word in each sentence.

7. _____

8. _____

9. _____

10. _____

11. _____

12. _____

# WORDS AT WORK

## Challenge Yourself

**frail   agent   maintain   contain**

Use your Spelling Dictionary to answer these questions. Then write sentences showing that you understand the meaning of each Challenge Word.

1. Would a bridge made of toothpicks be <u>frail</u>?

2. Could a secret <u>agent</u> work for a government?

3. Is it important to <u>maintain</u> a town's bridges and roads?

4. Are jars that <u>contain</u> jam empty?

## Write to the Point

Every village or town has rules to protect people, the things they own, and the environment. Make a list of rules for the children of "The Happy Village" to follow. Use spelling words from this lesson in your list.

**Challenge** Use one or more of the Challenge Words in your list.

## Proofreading

Use the marks to show the errors in the sentences below. Write the four misspelled words correctly in the blanks.

1. Our class was abel to make many things out of paper.

2. we made a boat with a sale on the table in Mr. Santiago's room.

3. Ms. Digg's class made a train that that was ate feet long.

4. We could not wate to paint it.

| | |
|---|---|
| ⬭ | word is misspelled |
| ≡ | letter should be capitalized |
| ⟋ | take out word |

1. _____

2. _____

3. _____

4. _____

21

# Lesson 4 Words with /ĕ/

**Listen for /ĕ/ as you say each word.**

dress

address

end

second

forget

spent

egg

next

help

test

head

read

ready

said

again

says

1. Write three words that have double consonants.

   gg _____     ss _____

   dd and ss _____

2. Which word begins and ends with the letter s?

   _____

3. Write two words in which ai spells /ĕ/.

   _____     _____

4. Write two words that end with the letters nd.

   _____

5. Write three words in which ea spells /ĕ/.

   _____     _____

   _____

6. Which four words end with the letter t?

   _____     _____

   _____     _____

7. Which word ends with the letter p?

   _____

8. Write the word that ends with the letter y.

   _____

22

# Checkpoint

Write a spelling word for each clue.
Then use the Checkpoint Study Plan on page 224.

1. I come right after you, so I'm ____ .

2. For breakfast you might eat an ____ .

3. I say, you say, he ____ .

4. If Eddie is all set to go, then Eddie is ____ .

5. The opposite of the beginning is the ____ .

6. To aid someone is to ____ .

7. If you used your money, your money is ____ .

8. "Once more" means ____ .

9. Next after first comes ____ .

10. The opposite of remember is ____ .

11. Something to wear is a ____ .

12. The past tense of say is ____ .

13. Mail is sent to your ____ .

14. This is the best book I have ____ .

15. Another word for quiz or exam is ____ .

16. Do you know what raining cats and dogs
    means? It means that it's raining heavily. A
    phrase like raining cats and dogs is called an
    idiom. You may know what each word of an
    idiom means. But that won't tell you what the
    whole idiom means. To keep one's ____ means
    to stay calm. To lose one's ____ means to lose
    one's calm. What is the mystery word? ____

23

# ME-2

Use each word once to complete this story.

ME-2 was a little robot with a big problem. She had a very bad memory.

Friday morning ME-2 ate bread and a scrambled _____. Then she forgot that she had eaten breakfast. So she ate it _____.

On Saturday she put on blue jeans. Then she forgot what she was wearing. So she put on her best _____, too.

Things were bad at home. And they were no better at school. When ME-2 remembered her reading book, she forgot what she had _____. When she remembered her math _____, she forgot to study. And she was never _____ for gym because she always forgot her sneakers.

One day ME-2 forgot where she lived. She had forgotten her own _____. So ME-2 _____ the night with her best friend, US-2. Her mother was very worried. She found ME-2 at school the very _____ day. Mother _____, "This won't happen a _____ time. You are going to go to the doctor."

The doctor gave ME-2 a checkup. Soon it was over. ME-2 told her mother, "The doctor _____ I'm just fine. I wish I could remember why you brought me here."

"Doctor, how can ME-2 be fine?" asked her mother. "She would lose her _____ if it was not screwed on her shoulders! Can't you _____ her?"

Her words gave the doctor an idea. The doctor looked at the screws in ME-2's head. Sure enough! One screw was loose. She fixed it. That put an _____ to ME-2's bad memory.

"Oh, no! I just remembered something," cried ME-2. "We get report cards tomorrow. That is something I wish I could _____!"

25

dress
address
end
second
forget
spent
egg
next
help
test
head
read
ready
said
again
says

# Entry Words and Entries

An entry word in a dictionary tells how a word is spelled. An entry word is printed in dark, heavy letters. The entry comes next. It gives more information about the word. Many words have more than one meaning. Different meanings are numbered.

> **read·y** | rĕd′ē | — *adjective* **readier, readiest** **1.** Prepared for action or use: *Are you ready to go? Dinner is ready.* **2.** Willing: *I'm ready to listen to your idea.* **3.** About to do something; likely: *She looked like she was ready to cry.* **4.** Quick; prompt and alert: *She has a ready answer for everything.* **5.** Easy to get at; close at hand: *You should always have some ready money.*

 Answer these questions about the dictionary entry above.

**1.** What is the entry word in the example above? _____

**2.** How many meanings does this word have? _____

 Write the following words in alphabetical order. Then look them up in the Spelling Dictionary. Write the page on which the entry appears. Then write the number of meanings each word has.

**egg    next    address    help**

| Word | Page | Number of Meanings |
|------|------|--------------------|
| **3.** _____ | _____ | _____ |
| **4.** _____ | _____ | _____ |
| **5.** _____ | _____ | _____ |
| **6.** _____ | _____ | _____ |

## Challenge Yourself

celebration       attempt

      genuine       athletic

What do you think each underlined Challenge Word means? Check your Spelling Dictionary to see if you are right. Then write sentences showing that you understand the meaning of each Challenge Word.

1. They had a <u>celebration</u> when ME-2 got a good report card.

2. The doctor's first <u>attempt</u> to help ME-2 did not work.

3. ME-2 was a <u>genuine</u> robot.

4. She liked gym class because she was <u>athletic</u>.

## Write to the Point

Sometimes it may be hard to remember all the things you have to do each day. You can help yourself remember by making a list. Make a list of things you have to do before and after school each day. Use spelling words from this lesson in your list.

**Challenge** Use one or more of the Challenge Words in your list.

## Proofreading

Use the marks to show the errors in the sentences below. Write the four misspelled words correctly in the blanks.

| | |
|---|---|
| ⬯ | word is misspelled |
| ⊙ | period is missing |
| ≡ | letter should be capitalized |

1. I often forgit things.

2. Mom sez i have to use my head.

3. here's a trick that will hulp.

4. Tie a bow on my secend finger

1. _____

2. _____

3. _____

4. _____

27

# Lesson 5　Plurals

**Say each word.**

clowns

trains

tests

eggs

hammers

paints

hands

papers


tables

places

pages

apples


classes

addresses

dresses

matches

Complete the word equations.

1. test + s =

2. egg + s =

3. train + s =

4. hand + s =

5. paint + s =

6. clown + s =

7. paper + s =

8. hammer + s =


9. page + s =

10. table + s =

11. place + s =

12. apple + s =


13. class + es =

14. dress + es =

15. match + es =

16. address + es =

28

# Checkpoint

Write a spelling word for each clue.
Then use the Checkpoint Study Plan on page 224.

1. Fruits that grow on trees are ____.

2. Pieces of clothing are ____.

3. Letters in the mail have names and ____.

4. Things to write on are ____.

5. Circus people who make you laugh are ____.

6. The woods and the sea are different ____.

7. You catch a basketball with your ____.

8. A book is made up of many ____.

9. Make a picture of a rainbow with many ____.

10. Things that run on railroad tracks are ____.

11. Hens lay, and you might eat, ____.

12. Are you taking one class or two ____?

13. Things you use to start fires are ____.

14. Tools you use with nails are ____.

15. The teacher will mark your ____.

16. This mystery word comes from the Latin word *tabula*. A *tabula* was a board or plank. It was often used for writing or playing games. The mystery word that comes from *tabula* names something we set our food on or play games on. Can you guess it? Add <u>s</u> to this word. What do you get? ____

# JOHN HENRY

All the people in the South knew about John Henry. They said he could swing a hammer so fast that you could hear thunder behind it. John Henry didn't go to _____ to learn how to swing a hammer. People said he was born with a hammer in his hand.

John Henry spent all of his time hammering steel spikes for the trains. He followed the _____ all over. He lived at many different _____ .

People will never forget the day John Henry raced a machine. It was one of the biggest _____ of his power. People came from _____ far away to see if John Henry could beat a machine. The women wore bright

_____. Men wore their best

shirts. They brought picnics of fresh bread and

_____. There were _____

for dessert. They sat on blankets or at picnic

_____.

The contest began. Who would win? Wham!
Wham! John Henry was fast. But the machine was
faster than John Henry.

"Bring me two _____!" he
cried. With hammers in both _____,
he was as fast as any machine. The hammers got
very hot. Soon they started to glow. They were like

_____.

"Look!" a woman shouted. "John Henry is
winning."

It was true. The smoke was gone. The people
saw that the man had beaten the machine.

John Henry isn't in the _____
of your history book. But people in the South still
talk about the greatest steel-driver of them all.

---

**A.** clown + clown = _____

**B.** paint + paint = _____

**C.** paper + paper = _____

*clowns*
*trains*
*tests*
*eggs*
*hammers*
*paints*
*hands*
*papers*
*tables*
*places*
*pages*
*apples*
*classes*
*addresses*
*dresses*
*matches*

# Base Words

A word from which other words are formed is called a base word.

*The base word for places is place.*
*The base word for tests is test.*

★Write the following words in alphabetical order. Then write the base word for each word.

**classes    eggs    addresses    hands**

Words                                    Base Words

1. _____            _____

2. _____            _____

3. _____            _____

4. _____            _____

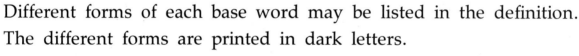

In a dictionary, many entry words are base words. To find the word <u>matches</u>, look up the base word <u>match</u>. To find the word <u>papers</u>, look up the base word <u>paper</u>.

Different forms of each base word may be listed in the definition. The different forms are printed in dark letters.

> **clown** | kloun | — *noun, plural* **clowns 1.** A person who has a job, usually with a circus, doing tricks and telling jokes to make people laugh: *a circus clown.* **2.** A person who is always making jokes or acting foolishly: *the class clown.*—*verb* **clowned, clowning 1.** To perform as a clown in a circus or show: *The chimpanzees clowned in the center ring of the circus.* **2.** To behave like a clown: *My friend clowns around too much.*

★Look at the dictionary entry above.

5. What is the base word? _____

6. What different forms are printed in dark letters?

_____            _____

# WORDS AT WORK

## Challenge Yourself

**losses  meteors  caverns  neckties**

Decide which Challenge Word fits each clue. Check your Spelling Dictionary to see if you were right. Then write sentences showing that you understand the meaning of each Challenge Word.

1. These look like bright streaks of light in the sky.

2. This word is made from two small words put together.

3. These can make ball players sad.

4. You might find bats in these.

## Write to the Point

The contest between John Henry and the machine was exciting. Make a sign to tell people about a contest. The contest can be real or make-believe. Tell what it is and when and where it will be. Use spelling words from this lesson in your sign.

**Challenge** Use one or more of the Challenge Words in your sign.

## Proofreading

Use the marks to show the errors in the sentences below. Write the four misspelled words correctly in the blanks.

| | |
|---|---|
| ⬭ | word is misspelled |
| ⊙ | period is missing |
| ☰ | letter should be capitalized |

1. Paul Bunyan had handes big enough to hold two trains

2. many paiges have been written about him.

3. He helped people who lived in different plases

4. You might have read about Paul Bunyan in one of your clases.

1. _____

2. _____

3. _____

4. _____

# Lesson 6    Words in Review

**A.** catch
   half
   laugh

**B.** place
   gray
   break
   April

**C.** afraid
   danger
   weigh
   they

**D.** address
   second
   ready
   again
   says

★ Use a piece of paper for the starred activities.

1. In Lesson 1 you studied two ways to spell /ă/: **a, au.** Write the words in list A.

2. In Lesson 2 you studied four ways to spell /ā/: **a_e, ay, ea, a.** Write the words in list B.

★3. Write the review words from lists A and B in alphabetical order.

4. In Lesson 3 you studied four ways to spell /ā/: **ai, a, ei, ey.** Write the words in list C.

5. In Lesson 4 you studied four ways to spell /ĕ/: **e, ea, ai, ay.** Write the words in list D.

★6. Now write a sentence for each review word in lists C and D.

★7. Write the review words in lists C and D in alphabetical order.

# Writer's Workshop

## A Personal Narrative

A personal narrative is a true story about you. A personal narrative often has words like I, me, we, and my. The beginning of a personal narrative should grab a reader's attention. Here is Rosa's personal narrative about her first job.

### My First Job

My first job taught me a big lesson. Mrs. Chen offered me ten dollars. All I had to do was carry magazines from her basement to a garbage can in her yard. "Sure!" I said. The next day, Mrs. Chen showed me her basement. Magazines took up every bit of space. It took me two weeks to carry them all out! Now when someone offers me a job, I get all the facts before I say "Sure!"

To write her personal narrative, Rosa followed the steps in the writing process. She began with a **Prewriting** activity to plan what she would write. Rosa used a chain of events chart to list the things that happened. Rosa's chain of events chart is shown here. Study what Rosa did.

| 1 | 2 | 3 |
|---|---|---|
| Mrs. Chen offered me $10 to carry magazines. | Her basement was full of magazines. | The job took two weeks. |

**It's Your Turn**

Get ready to write your own personal narrative. It can be about the first time you did something or about another special event in your life. After you have decided what to write about, make a chain of events chart. Then follow the other steps in the writing process—**Writing**, **Revising**, **Proofreading**, and **Publishing**.

# Lesson 7    Words with /ĕ/

**Listen for /ĕ/ as you say each word.**

best

better

cents

February

never

kept

sent

September

slept

them

then

Wednesday

when

friend

many

guess

1. Which three words end with the letters <u>er</u>?

_____    _____

2. Which word begins with the letter <u>m</u>?

_____

3. In which two words do you see two vowels together but hear only one vowel sound?

_____    _____

4. Which two words begin with the letters <u>th</u>?

_____    _____

5. Which three words are always spelled with a capital letter? _____

_____    _____

6. Write the word that begins with the letters <u>wh</u>.

_____

7. Which four words begin with /s/?

_____    _____

_____    _____

8. Write two words that end with the last three letters of <u>swept</u>.

_____    _____

9. Which word ends with the letters <u>st</u>?

# Checkpoint

Write a spelling word for each clue.
Then use the Checkpoint Study Plan on page 224.

1. The opposite of few is ____.

2. "Not ever" means ____.

3. Valentine's Day is in ____.

4. The past tense of send is ____.

5. Someone you know and like is your ____.

6. When you don't know the answer, try to ____.

7. "Held on to and saved" means ____.

8. School starts in ____.

9. Tonight you'll sleep, last night you ____.

10. The finest is the ____.

11. You ask what, why, where, and ____.

12. The day that follows Tuesday is ____.

13. They got lost, and we found ____.

14. More excellent than another is ____.

15. It didn't happen now, but ____.

16. The mystery word comes from the Latin word *centum*. *Centum* means hundred. Other words also come from *centum*. One hundred years is called a century. A bug with one hundred legs is called a centipede. In Mexico, one hundred centavos make a peso. In America, one hundred ____ make a dollar. Can you guess the mystery word? ____

37

# Capitals

Use a capital letter to begin the names of people and pets and for the word I.

*Adam* and *I* read a book about a dog named *Dominic*.
A raccoon named *Macaroon* is in a book by *Julia Cunningham*.

★ In the sentences below, find each word that should begin with a capital letter. Then write the sentence correctly. Draw a circle around any spelling words in your sentences.

1. c.w. anderson wrote books about a horse named blaze.

2. blaze was kept by a boy named billy.

3. a horse named thunderbolt became friends with billy and blaze.

4. old yeller is the book i like best.

5. old yeller belonged to travis.

6. faithful is the word for old yeller.

★ Think of stories you have read.

7. Write the names of animals from these stories.

# WORDS AT WORK

## Challenge Yourself

**sketch index blend friendliness**

Decide which Challenge Word fits each clue. Check your Spelling Dictionary to see if you were right. Then write sentences showing that you understand the meaning of each Challenge Word.

1. When you do this, you mix things.

2. This makes people feel liked.

3. You can use this to look up something in a book.

4. It helps to do one before you make a final drawing.

## Write to the Point

People often put up signs when they lose a pet. Make a sign to help Carlos find Lily. Describe Lily, tell when she was lost, and give a phone number to call. You can even offer a reward. Use spelling words from this lesson in your sign.

**Challenge** Use one or more of the Challenge Words in your sign.

## Proofreading

Use the marks to show the errors in the sentences below. Write the four misspelled words correctly in the blanks.

| | |
|---|---|
| ⬭ | word is misspelled |
| ⊙ | period is missing |
| ☰ | letter should be capitalized |

1. My frend Kim has many fish.

2. she keeps thim in a tank.

3. Last Febuary Kim went to florida.

4. Then I kep the fish at my house

1. _____

2. _____

3. _____

4. _____

# Lesson 8    Words with /ē/

**Listen for /ē/ as you say each word.**

meet

need

sleep

street

queen

wheel

free

sneeze


dream

each

meat

read

sea

team

please


people

1. Write the word that begins with a vowel.

_____

2. Write two words that sound alike but are not spelled the same.

_____  _____

3. Write two words that end with the last three letters of <u>cream</u>.

_____  _____

4. Write two words that end with /z/.

_____  _____

5. Which two words end with two vowel letters?

_____  _____

6. Write the word that begins with the letters <u>qu</u>.

_____

7. Write two words that end with the letter <u>d</u>.

_____  _____

8. Which word begins with the letters <u>st</u>?

_____

9. Write two words that end with /l/.

_____

10. Which word ends with the letter <u>p</u>?

# Checkpoint

Write a spelling word for each clue.
Then use the Checkpoint Study Plan on page 224.

1. If you don't have to pay, it's ——.

2. Human beings are ——.

3. A plane is to fly, a book is to ——.

4. Something to eat is ——.

5. When you have a cold, you might ——.

6. When you ask for something, say ——.

7. "Every single one" means ——.

8. Nine baseball players make a ——.

9. When you must have something, you —— it.

10. Another word for ocean is ——.

11. When you are tired, you go to ——.

12. To come face to face is to ——.

13. Something that rolls is a ——.

14. A nightmare is a bad ——.

15. A road is a ——.

16. Sometimes the meaning of a word changes.
    This mystery word comes from the Old English
    word *cwen.* Long ago in England, *cwen* meant
    wife. Later it was used for only one special
    wife. She was the wife or *cwen* of the king.
    Guess the mystery word. Then you'll know
    what we say today instead of *cwen.* ——

Use each word once to complete this story.

# Queen of the Roads

Many years ago, in a castle by the _____,

there lived a beautiful _____. She was a

good queen. The _____ in her

kingdom loved her. Her life was easy. But she was

unhappy because _____ day was just like

the day before. Each morning she would sit and

_____ the news of the day. Each afternoon

she would _____ with her advisers. Every

night she had a dinner of roasted _____,

hot cider, and sweet fruits.

But this did not _____ her.

Every night when she went to _____

she would _____ of leaving the castle.

"I _____ a change," the queen thought.

One day she told a servant, "Today I want to be

_____. Get a _____ of horses and

a carriage ready for me."

The queen got in the carriage. She rode alone.

She drove down the main _____.

All the people saw her and cheered.

44

"This will never do," she said. So she headed for the country. Suddenly, the carriage hit a big rock. A _____ flew off. The carriage was very heavy. The queen could not fix the wheel alone. It was getting dark and cold. She began to shake and _____.

At last, two farmers came by. They helped the queen fix the wheel.

"Will you please give us a favor in return?" one farmer asked the queen.

"Anything you wish," the happy queen said.

"Build a new road so other carriages won't hit the rocks."

"It will be done," answered the queen. "I shall build new roads all over my kingdom!"

And the queen was so busy keeping her promise that she was never unhappy again.

45

*meet*
*need*
*sleep*
*street*
*queen*
*wheel*
*free*
*sneeze*
*dream*
*each*
*meat*
*read*
*sea*
*team*
*please*
*people*

# Nouns

A noun is a word that names a person, place, thing, or idea.

*boy    city    toy    beauty*
*girl    town    dog    peace*

⭐ Write the noun in each group of words below.

1. walked    meat    up          2. queen    over    helping

_____

3. ran    into    street          4. people    like    about

_____

5. read    sea    swam          6. until    team    each

_____

⭐ Decide which noun fits each unfinished sentence. Then write the sentence.

**sneeze    wheel    sea    dream    people    street**

7. I had a wonderful ___ last night.

_____

8. All the ___ who live on my ___ were in it.

_____

_____

9. We sailed out to ___ in a big ship.

_____

10. My little sister steered the ___ of the ship.

_____

_____

11. I woke up from my dream when I heard a loud ___!

_____

_____

46

## Challenge Yourself

**deceive    feat    seam    teenager**

What do you think each underlined Challenge Word means? Check your Spelling Dictionary to see if you are right. Then write sentences showing that you understand the meaning of each Challenge Word.

1. An honest queen would not <u>deceive</u> the people in her kingdom.

2. The young knight performed a brave <u>feat</u>.

3. I ripped the <u>seam</u> in my jacket.

4. I will be a <u>teenager</u> when I am thirteen.

## Write to the Point

The queen needed a change. She wanted to be free and to visit a new place. Write a paragraph about a place you have visited or would like to visit. Use exact words to make your paragraph interesting. Use spelling words from this lesson in your paragraph.

**Challenge** Use one or more of the Challenge Words in your paragraph.

## Proofreading

Use the marks to show the errors in the sentences below. Write the four misspelled words correctly in the blanks.

| | |
|---|---|
| ◯ | word is misspelled |
| ⊙ | period is missing |
| ⚋ | take out word |

1. A quene had a a strange dream.

2. She was on a baseball teme.

3. A sea of of peeple cheered.

4. She wanted to meat each fan

1. _____

2. _____

3. _____

4. _____

# Lesson 9    Words with /ē/

Listen for /ē/ as you say each word.

happy
funny
very
busy
sleepy
carry
sunny
every
family
penny
only
city
story

these
even

key

1. Which three words begin with a vowel?

_____

_____

2. Which two words begin with /k/?

_____

3. Write the two words in which you hear /z/ but do not see the letter z.

_____

4. Write five words that have double consonants.

nn _____        nn _____

nn _____        pp _____

rr _____

5. Write the word in which you hear /ē/ in both syllables. _____

6. Which two words end with the letters ery?

_____

7. Which two words begin with the letter f?

_____

8. Which word ends with the last three letters of glory? _____

9. Write the word in which you hear /s/ but do not see the letter s. _____

# Checkpoint

Write a spelling word for each clue.
Then use the Checkpoint Study Plan on page 224.

1. If it's just one, it's the one and ___.

2. If you can't pick it up, it's too heavy to ___.

3. A fairy tale is a kind of ___.

4. "Smooth, not rough" means ___.

5. A clown tries to make you laugh by being ___.

6. If you feel like taking a nap, you're ___.

7. If you have a lot of work to do, you're ___.

8. The opposite of sad is ___.

9. "Each one" means ___.

10. You open a lock with a ___.

11. A room that is full of sunlight is ___.

12. It's not those, but ___.

13. The test was ___ hard.

14. One cent is a ___.

15. A large town is a ___.

16. Long ago in Rome, rich people had many
servants. Men servants were called *famuli*.
Women servants were called *famulae*. Together
they were called *familia*. Later, a husband, a
wife, their children, and their servants were
called a *familia*. Can you guess the mystery
word that comes from *familia*? ___

49

Use each word once to complete these pages.

# The Whole Tooth and Nothing But...

It all began on a bright, _____ day.

My brother Johnny is _____ six years old.

He dared me to pull out my loose tooth. He said

he would _____ my books to school for

a week if I did. I love my family very much. I

_____ love Johnny. But I don't let anyone

in my _____ call me a coward.

So I tied one end of a string around my dog

Red's collar. Red didn't look very _____

about it. In fact, he was _____, so I

had to wake him up. I was ready to tie the other

end around my tooth. Just then Fishstick, our cat,

ran in front of us. And Red ran after her.

The string got caught on my finger. And I was pulled along after Red. People stopped to laugh at us. We must have looked pretty _____ . Then Fishstick jumped up on an apple cart. Red jumped, too. When Red landed on the cart, _____ apple rolled into the street.

Just then, a masked man ran out of the bank. He was too _____ running to notice _____ apples. He went slipping and sliding. Before we knew it, the police had him.

Then I noticed that my tooth was missing. And I didn't even know where it had gone.

The next day, I read this _____ in the newspaper:

# TROUBLE AT PENNY BANK

Friday began as a quiet day in the _____ . Then a small girl, a big dog, and a cat turned over an apple cart in front of the _____ Bank. This was the _____ in the capture of Mr. X.

When asked how it felt to be a hero, Cissy Thomas said, "It's _____ nice. But has anyone found a missing tooth?"

51

happy
funny
very
busy
sleepy
carry
sunny
every
family
penny
only
city
story
these
even
key

# Alphabetical Order

The words in a dictionary are in alphabetical order.

⭐ Look at the Spelling Dictionary at the back of this book. Then complete these sentences.

1. Words that begin with **A** start on page _____ and end on page _____.

2. Words that begin with **K** start on page _____ and end on page _____.

3. Words that begin with **S** start on page _____ and end on page _____.

⭐ Write the words below in alphabetical order. Then find each one in the Spelling Dictionary and write the number of the page it is on.

funny    even    carry    key

| Words | Page | | Words | Page |
|-------|------|---|-------|------|
| 4. _____ | _____ | 5. | _____ | _____ |
| 6. _____ | _____ | 7. | _____ | _____ |

⭐ Write this story. Use these words in alphabetical order for the missing words in the story. You will need to capitalize one word.

**very    story    only    city    busy    family    happy    penny    these**

Cindy had a _____ Saturday. She went to the _____ with her _____. The city always made her _____. But there was _____ so much she could do in a day. Her mom took her to the _____ arcade. They also went to a children's theater to hear a _____.

_____ were the two things she liked best in the city. Was she tired when she got home? Yes, _____!

## Challenge Yourself

**misery   scheme   soggy   cemetery**

What do you think each underlined Challenge Word means? Check your Spelling Dictionary to see if you are right. Then write sentences showing that you understand the meaning of each Challenge Word.

1. A headache can cause <u>misery</u>.

2. The children had a <u>scheme</u> for raising money to buy a gift.

3. Mia changed her <u>soggy</u> clothes after she fell in a puddle.

4. Some grave markers in the <u>cemetery</u> are very old.

## Write to the Point

Write a paragraph about losing a tooth. It can be a true story, or it can be made up. Your paragraph can be about you or someone you know. It can be funny, or it can be serious. Use spelling words from this lesson in your paragraph.

**Challenge** Use one or more of the Challenge Words in your paragraph.

## Proofreading

Use the marks to show the errors in the sentences below. Write the four misspelled words correctly in the blanks.

| | |
|---|---|
| ⬭ | word is misspelled |
| ⊙ | period is missing |
| ≡ | letter should be capitalized |

1. Cissy's famly was proud of her.

2. Eavn Johnny said she was a hero.

3. Mayor wang heard the storie.

4. she gave Cissy a kee to the city

1. _____

2. _____

3. _____

4. _____

Use each word once to complete this story.

# Face the Music

It was June, the last _____ of
school. And this was the last weekend before
_____ vacation. Josh's favorite day
was Sunday. But not this _____ .

Yesterday Josh had found two dollars in his
jacket. He could not remember where the money
came _____ . But he knew how
_____ he wanted a record. So he bought
the record with the _____ .

Today he remembered! The two dollars was class
money. The _____ kids had given him
the money to buy Mr. Farar, the music teacher, a
class present.

Josh didn't have any more money. And the
record had been on sale. He couldn't return it.
What could he do?

Josh was sad. His _____ asked
what was wrong. He was so ashamed, he said,
"It's _____ ."

Then Patty called. "How _____ Mr.
Farar's present look?"

56

"Well . . ." Josh began.

"Remember to put a note on it. Don't forget all of our names."

Josh hung up the telephone. But Patty's words had given him a great idea. He found his clay _____ his bed. He formed the clay into an egg shape and stuck a stick into it. Josh dried it in the _____ . Later he painted it silver.

_____ morning it was dry. He wrapped it and took it to school.

At noon he went to _____ . Patty asked, "Where's the present and the note?"

"You'll see," said Josh.

Mr. Farar opened his gift in _____ of the class. "A record album and a silver music note with your names on it!" he exclaimed. "This took _____ a lot of work. This is one note I'll hold forever!"

mother
front
month
money
from
other
nothing
Monday
such
summer
much
lunch
sun
under
Sunday
does

# Question Marks

Use a question mark (?) at the end of a sentence that asks a question.

*Does Carlo like riddles?*
*Can he answer these?*

★ Help Carlo answer these riddles. Copy each riddle. Be sure to add a question mark or a period. Then choose an answer.

## Answers

**a sponge**     **her lap**     **your teeth**     **the letter m**

1. What comes once in a month, twice in a moment, and never in a hundred years _____

_____

Answer: _____

2. What does your friend lose whenever she stands up _____

_____

_____

Answer: _____

3. What is full of holes and still holds water _____

_____

Answer: _____

4. What can you put into the apple pie you have for lunch _____

_____

Answer: _____

58

# WORDS AT WORK

## Challenge Yourself

**huddle buzzard somebody frontier**

Decide which Challenge Word fits each clue. Check your Spelling Dictionary to see if you were right. Then write sentences showing that you understand the meaning of each Challenge Word.

1. We use this word to talk about a person we don't know.

2. It is a large bird with a beak.

3. It is a place where few people live.

4. Football players make one of these to plan their next move.

## Write to the Point

Josh made a gift for Mr. Farar out of clay. Think of a gift you can make out of things you have at home or school. Then write a paragraph telling what your gift will be and how you plan to make it. Use spelling words from this lesson in your paragraph.

**Challenge** Use one or more of the Challenge Words in your paragraph.

## Proofreading

Use the marks to show the errors in the sentences below. Write the four misspelled words correctly in the blanks.

1. Josh can't wait for for somer.

2. He enjoys being in the son

3. Some days he plays in his frunt yard.

4. Other days he does nuthin much.

| | |
|---|---|
| ◯ | word is misspelled |
| ⊙ | period is missing |
| ✎ | take out word |

1. _____

2. _____

3. _____

4. _____

59

# Lesson 11 Contractions

**Say each word.**

they'll
she'll
I'll
we'll
you'll

I've
we've
you've
they've

he's
she's
it's

I'd
you'd
they'd

I'm

1. Write the word that sounds exactly like <u>weave</u>.

   _____

2. Write the word that sounds exactly like <u>its</u>.

   _____

3. Write the word that sounds exactly like <u>aisle</u>.

   _____

4. Which three words have the <u>ey</u> spelling of /ā/?

   _____    _____

5. Which five words have the <u>e</u> spelling of /ē/?

   _____    _____

   _____

6. Write the four words that always begin with a capital letter.

   _____    _____

   _____    _____

7. Write the three words that begin with the letter <u>y</u>.

   _____    _____

# Checkpoint

Write a spelling word for each clue.
Then use the Checkpoint Study Plan on page 224.

1. she + will = ___

2. we + will = ___

3. I + will = ___

4. you + will = ___

5. they + will = ___

6. I + have = ___

7. they + have = ___

8. we + have = ___

9. you + have = ___

10. she + is = ___

11. it + is = ___

12. he + is = ___

13. they + would = ___

14. you + would = ___

15. I + am = ___

16. Verbs have different forms for past, present, and future action. Long ago, English verbs used to have even more forms. A few of these forms are still used today. The mystery word is a special form of the verb <u>will</u>. It used to be spelled *wolde*. Guess how we spell *wolde* today. Then make a contraction with the word <u>I</u> to get the mystery word. ___

61

Use each word once to complete this story.

# DIARY OF A DETECTIVE -
## CASE #13

I went over to Pete's house for dinner. The first thing he said was, "We are having roast beef. _____ defrosting in the kitchen right now."

I know Pete. And _____ always hungry. I'm not. _____ rather work on a mystery than eat.

We were in the yard. Then we heard a loud bang inside the house. "_____ sure it's not Mom. _____ still at work. _____ be home in an hour."

We ran to the house. The back door was wide open. In the kitchen, a chair was on its side. In the hall, my coat was on the floor. We heard a strange noise upstairs. "Let's go next door and call the police," whispered Pete. "_____ know what to do. _____ handled lots of burglars."

I didn't think it was burglars because _____ be very quiet. Then I noticed something. "_____ got it!" I yelled.

"Ssh!" said Pete. "If you are not quiet,

_____ scare them off!"

"Together _____ be able to handle this,"
I said. "_____ got all the clues we need.
Look around."

Pete looked. Then he said, "The beef is missing!
What kind of burglar would take a piece of meat?
And look at the floor. Where did those paw prints
come from?"

Before I could answer, a puppy came down the
steps. He barked at us.

Pete laughed. He said, "Well, puppy. I see that
_____ eaten our dinner. Now I suppose
_____ like some dessert."

The dog just wagged his tail. He trotted out the
door. But _____ bet he was happy.

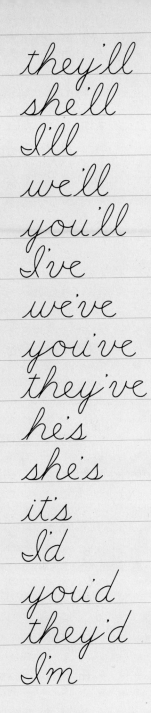

*they'll*
*she'll*
*I'll*
*we'll*
*you'll*
*I've*
*we've*
*you've*
*they've*
*he's*
*she's*
*it's*
*I'd*
*you'd*
*they'd*
*I'm*

# Apostrophes

A contraction is one word made from two words. It is easier and quicker to say than the two words. A contraction has at least one letter and sound left out. An apostrophe (') shows where those letters have been left out.

| Two Words | Contraction | Left Out |
|-----------|-------------|----------|
| *I am* | *I'm* | *a* |
| *we have* | *we've* | *ha* |

⭐ Write the contraction for each set of words. Then write the letters that you left out.

| Two Words | Contraction | Left Out |
|-----------|-------------|----------|
| 1. they will | | |
| 2. she has | | |
| 3. it is | | |
| 4. she will | | |
| 5. he is | | |
| 6. you have | | |
| 7. I have | | |

⭐ Choose four contractions and use each one in a sentence.

8. _____

9. _____

10. _____

11. _____

## Challenge Yourself

**would've could've who'll where'd**

Use your Spelling Dictionary to answer these questions. Then write sentences showing that you understand the meaning of each Challenge Word.

1. Is <u>would've</u> a contraction for <u>would have</u>?

2. Is <u>could've</u> a contraction for <u>could give</u>?

3. Is <u>who'll</u> a contraction for <u>who all</u>?

4. Is <u>where'd</u> a contraction for <u>where did</u>?

## Write to the Point

Think about detectives you know from books or television. Decide what makes these people good detectives. Write a paragraph telling why you or someone else would be a good detective. Use spelling words from this lesson in your paragraph.

**Challenge** Use one or more of the Challenge Words in your paragraph.

## Proofreading

Use the marks to show the errors in the sentences below. Write the four misspelled words correctly in the blanks.

| ⬭ | word is misspelled |
| ⊙ | period is missing |
| ≡ | letter should be capitalized |

1. I'me not sure whose puppy they've found.

2. Pete thought you'ld know.

3. We'v asked all our neighbors

4. ann says i'ts from the next town

1. _____

2. _____

3. _____

4. _____

# Lesson 12 Words in Review

**A.** slept

friend

many

guess

**B.** meet

queen

team

please

people

**C.** family

these

even

key

**D.** month

such

does

★Use a piece of paper for the starred activities.

**1.** In Lesson 7 you studied four ways to spell /ĕ/: **e, ie, a, ue.** Write the words in list A.

_____ _____

_____ _____

**2.** In Lesson 8 you studied three ways to spell /ē/: **ee, ea, eo.** Write the words in list B.

_____ _____

_____ _____

_____ _____

★**3.** Now write a sentence for each review word in lists A and B.

**4.** In Lesson 9 you studied three more ways to spell /ē/: **y, e, ey.** Write the words in list C.

_____ _____

_____ _____

**5.** In Lesson 10 you studied three ways to spell /ŭ/: **o, u, oe.** Write the words in list D.

_____ _____

★**6.** Write the review words in lists C and D. Look up each word in the Spelling Dictionary and write the sound spelling next to each word.

★**7.** Now, put all the words in lists A and B in alphabetical order.

# Writer's Workshop

## A Narrative

A narrative is a story. Every good story has a beginning, a middle, and an end. In the beginning of a story, writers tell who or what the story is about. They often tell where and when the story takes place. Here is the beginning of Leon's story about an unusual giraffe.

> ### The Mystery of the Talking Giraffe
> Ryan looked at Jan. "Did you hear that?" he asked in a trembling voice. Jan didn't answer. She just kept staring at the giraffe. Ryan and Jan lived only a block from the Davis City Zoo. They came every Saturday morning, all summer long. The zoo workers knew them by name. The animals seemed to recognize them. But none of the animals had ever said hello to them before.

To write his narrative, Leon followed the steps in the writing process. He began with a **Prewriting** activity using a story map. The map helped him decide what would happen at the beginning, middle, and end of his narrative. Leon's story map is shown here. Study what Leon did.

**Beginning**
Ryan and Jane hear a giraffe say hello.

**Middle**
They see a wire and speaker.

**End**
They discover the zookeeper's trick.

**It's Your Turn**

Get ready to write your own story. It can be an adventure story, a mystery like Leon's, or anything you choose. After you have decided what to write about, make a story map. Then follow the other steps in the writing process—**Writing, Revising, Proofreading,** and **Publishing.**

# Lesson 13  Words with /ŭ/

Listen for /ŭ/ as you say each word.

won

lovely

done

one

shove

some

something

cover

hundred

must

butter

supper

number

just

sum

1. Write four words that end with the letters er.

_____    _____

_____    _____

2. Which word is made up of two words put

   together? _____

3. Write two words beginning with the letter s that

   sound exactly alike but are not spelled alike.

   _____    _____

4. Write two other words that sound exactly alike

   but are spelled differently.

   _____    _____

5. Which two words end with the letters st?

   _____    _____

6. In which three words do you hear /v/?

   _____

   _____

7. Write three words that have the letters one.

   _____

   _____

8. Write the word that begins with the first three

   letters of hunt. _____

9. Write two words that have double consonants.

   pp _____    tt _____

# Checkpoint

Write a spelling word for each clue.
Then use the Checkpoint Study Plan on page 224.

1. "Push" means ____.

2. The opposite of all is ____.

3. Ten is a ____.

4. Another word for pretty is ____.

5. If you are completely finished, you're ____.

6. When you add numbers, the answer is the ____.

7. The opposite of nothing is ____.

8. The last meal of the day is ____.

9. Three minus two leaves ____.

10. If you have to, you ____.

11. One team lost, the other team ____.

12. The number after 99 is one ____.

13. More than none, but not all is ____.

14. The opposite of unjust is ____.

15. Another word for lid is ____.

16. This mystery word comes from the Greek word *bousturos*. *Bous* meant cow. *Turos* meant cheese. The Romans learned this word from the Greeks. But they changed the word to *butyrum*. Write the mystery word. ____

# Homophones

Words that sound alike but are spelled differently and have different meanings are called <u>homophones</u>. The following words are homophones. Do you know what each word means?

<u>one</u> and <u>won</u>
<u>some</u> and <u>sum</u>

★ Rewrite each sentence using a correct homophone from above in each blank. Use the Spelling Dictionary to find meanings.

1. Jack ____ two blue ribbons and ____ trophy.

_____

2. Jill found the ____ of ____ numbers.

_____

★ Use these homophones to write the following sentences.

| ate | son |
|-----|-----|
| eight | sun |

3. Jason ____ his supper. _____

_____

4. The ____ looked lovely after the rain. _____

_____

_____

5. We just met her daughter and her ____. _____

_____

6. My favorite number is ____. _____

_____

## Challenge Yourself

income    smudge    slump    instruct

What do you think each underlined Challenge Word means? Check your Spelling Dictionary to see if you are right. Then write sentences showing that you understand the meaning of each Challenge Word.

1. My allowance is my <u>income</u>.

2. The puppy's wet nose left a <u>smudge</u> on the window.

3. You will look taller if you don't <u>slump</u>.

4. I have a good teacher to <u>instruct</u> me in math.

## Write to the Point

Some people believe that doing your best is more important than winning. Do you agree? Write a paragraph about how important winning is to you. Give reasons why you think as you do. Use spelling words from this lesson in your paragraph.

**Challenge** Use one or more of the Challenge Words in your paragraph.

## Proofreading

Use the marks to show the errors in the sentences below. Write the four misspelled words correctly in the blanks.

| word is misspelled |
| letter should be capitalized |
| take out word |

1. stacey won a lovley ribbon.

2. She also got sum money.

3. It was was a hunderd dollars.

4. being nomber one must be fun!

1. _____

2. _____

3. _____

4. _____

73

# John and Apple Pie

The _____ of P.S. 103 wanted to plant trees. In the playground, Jessie and Evan talked about what kind of tree they wanted.

"I _____ we should plant a fir tree," said Evan. "It would stay green, even when it snows in _____." Evan kicked a ball to Jessie. They began to _____ the ball around the playground while they talked.

"Fir trees are _____," said Jessie. "But I think we should _____ with an apple tree, in honor of Johnny Appleseed."

"Who's Johnny Appleseed?" asked Evan.

"I've _____ reading about him," said Jessie. The children stopped playing. Jessie told Evan more. "His real name was John Chapman. He was born in Massachusetts. In 1800, he was in Pennsylvania and he crossed a big _____ to Ohio. He planted seeds along the way. Soon, _____ trees began to grow all over the countryside."

"Did he keep planting trees?" asked Evan.

"Yes. From January to _____ he planted them. He wanted to _____ America with apple orchards. He took loving care of the orchards _____ he planted. His trees blossomed every _____.

"Some people thought he was strange. He wore tattered clothing. Then he did a very special _____ that changed people's minds. During the War of 1812, he traveled many kilometers to warn American troops about an attack. Now what do you think about an apple tree?"

"You'll get my vote for an apple tree," said Evan.

"Did my story convince you?" asked Jessie.

"No," answered Evan. "I want an apple tree because apple pie is my favorite _____!"

Evan ran as Jessie threw the ball at him.

think
winter
children
dish
fill
little
thing
spring
kick
river
which
pretty
December
begin
been

# Capitals

The names of streets always begin with a capital letter. When the words <u>road</u>, <u>street</u>, and <u>avenue</u> come after the street name, they must begin with a capital, too.

*Pam Katz lives on <u>Wayside Street</u>.*
*What street do you live on?*

⭐ Study the map. Then write the answers.

1. Maria's house is on ____.

_____

2. The school is on ____.

_____

3. Enter the post office parking lot from ____.

_____

4. The three streets that border the park are ____, ____, and ____.

_____

_____

5. Enter the picnic area from ____.

_____

_____

6. The only café is called ____. It is on ____.

_____

_____

## Challenge Yourself

| spinach | luggage | width | arctic |

Decide which Challenge Word fits each clue. Check your Spelling Dictionary to see if you were right. Then write sentences showing that you understand the meaning of each Challenge Word.

1. Polar bears and some seals enjoy this kind of air.

2. It is a green vegetable.

3. It holds your clothes when you travel.

4. It is the distance from one side to the other.

## Write to the Point

Evan's favorite dish is apple pie. What is yours? Write a paragraph telling what your favorite or least favorite food is. Tell what you like most or least about it. Use exact words to describe the taste. Use spelling words from this lesson in your paragraph.

**Challenge** Use one or more of the Challenge Words in your paragraph.

## Proofreading

Use the marks to show the errors in the sentences below. Write the four misspelled words correctly in the blanks.

| ⬭ | word is misspelled |
| ⊙ | period is missing |
| = | letter should be capitalized |

1. In Decembur that tree is bare

2. you can see little buds in sprign.

3. White blossoms bigin to open

4. Then prittey red apples grow.

1. _____

2. _____

3. _____

4. _____

79

# Lesson 15 Words with /ī/

**Listen for /ī/ as you say each word.**

line

drive

inside

nice

shine

while

size

miles

write

mine

alike

times

white

tiny

lion

eyes

1. Write two words that begin and end with a vowel.

_____    _____

2. Which three words begin with the letter <u>w</u>?

_____

_____

3. Write the word that ends with /ē/.

_____

4. Which word begins with /s/ and ends with /z/?

_____

5. Write four words that end with /n/.

_____

_____

6. Which three words end with the letter <u>s</u>?

_____

_____

7. Write the word in which you hear /s/ but do not see the letter <u>s</u>. _____

8. Write the word that begins with the first three letters of <u>dried</u>. _____

9. In which word do you see the letter <u>e</u> twice?

_____

# Checkpoint

Write a spelling word for each clue.
Then use the Checkpoint Study Plan on page 224.

1. To make a car go is to ___.

2. "Very, very small" means ___.

3. "A little later" means in a little ___.

4. To measure long distances, we use ___.

5. "Not rude, but pleasant" means ___.

6. The sun and the stars ___.

7. You can use a ruler to draw a straight ___.

8. Something that belongs to me is ___.

9. A baby wears a small ___.

10. The opposite of outside is ___.

11. You use a pencil to ___.

12. You see with your ___.

13. Things that are the same are ___.

14. The color of snow is ___.

15. "Multiplied by" means ___.

16. This mystery word comes from the Greek word *lēon*. Many names come from this mystery word. Leona, Lenore, Leo, Leopold, and Lionel all come from it. The mystery word means a big, wild animal. Can you guess it? ___

Use each word once to complete this story.

# Just a BIG Cat

The lion belongs to the cat family. You might even say that a _____ is just a big cat.

A wild lion and a house cat are very much _____. They both have claws that they can pull _____ their paws. This keeps their claws _____ and sharp. Lions and house cats have _____ that see well in the dark. If a light should _____ on their eyes at night, their eyes will glow.

But lions are very different from house cats. The greatest difference is _____. A male lion

can weigh 500 pounds, _____ a house
cat will weigh about 10 pounds. A house cat seems
_____ next to a lion.

The lion's fur is brownish-yellow. This color
makes it easy for the lion to hide. A house cat can
be many colors. It can even be snowy _____ .

A male lion is the only cat that has a mane. The
mane makes him look bigger and stronger.

Lions live in groups called prides. At
_____ , as many as 35 lions may live in
a pride. These lions will hunt together. They usually
walk about five _____ a day.

Lions don't let other animals hunt on their land.
They roar as if to say, "Keep out! This land is
_____ ." That may be why the lion is called
"King of the Beasts."

Today, most lions live in Africa. But lions can be
seen in parks and zoos. People _____
from far away and stand in a long _____
to see a lion.

Many people _____ books about
lions. Even though people are afraid of lions, most
still think lions are beautiful animals.

83

line
drive
inside
nice
shine
while
size
miles
write
mine
alike
times
white
tiny
lion
eyes

# Guide Words

The two words in dark letters at the top of each dictionary page are called <u>guide words</u>. All the words on a dictionary page are arranged between the two guide words. The guide word at the left is the first word on the page. The other guide word is the last entry word on the page.

★ Look at this dictionary page.

**alike | be**

**a·like** | ə līk′ | —*adjective* Similar; like one another: *The goldfish in my fish tank all look alike.*

**al·most** | ôl′mōst′ | *or* | ôl mōst′ | —*adverb* Nearly: *It is almost time for lunch.*

**a·lone** | ə lōn′ | —*adjective* By oneself: *I like to walk by the sea all alone.*

**a·long** | ə lông′ | *or* | ə lŏng′ | —*preposition* Besid... We walked... ...le: To... ...y around. ...About; here and there: ...circus traveled around the country. | ärt | —*noun, plural* **arts** **1.** A painting, drawing, or sculpture. **2.** A skill or craft: *Dancing is an art.*

**ask** | ăsk | *or* | äsk | —*verb* **asked, asking** **1.** To put a question to: *I asked my father where he was born.* **2.** To request: *I asked for a small pizza.*

**ate** | āt | Look up **eat.** • **Ate** sounds like **eight.**

**Au·gust** | ô′gəst | —*noun* The eighth month of the year: *The weather is always so hot in Aug...*

**au·tu...** ...arns A farm ...used for storing grain and hay and for keeping livestock: *The farmer checked to see if his cows were in the barn.*

**be** | bē | —*helping* or *auxiliary verb* **was** | wŏz | *or* | wŭz | *or* | wəz |, **were** | wûr |, **been** | bĭn | Be is used as a helping verb with action words to show continuing action: *I was running as fast as I could, but Ida was winning. When will you be finished with the crayons? We were about to leave, when the telephone rang. Timmy has been gone for over two hours.*

197

**1.** What are the guide words? _____

and _____

**2.** What is the first entry word? _____

**3.** What is the last entry word? _____

★ Look up these spelling words in the dictionary at the back of the book. Write the guide words and page number for each.

<u>Guide Words</u>                <u>Page</u>

**4.** while _____

**5.** drive _____

**6.** nice _____

## Challenge Yourself

**variety    admire    chime    define**

Use your Spelling Dictionary to answer these questions. Then write sentences showing that you understand the meaning of each Challenge Word.

1. Would you find a <u>variety</u> of toys in a toy store?

2. Would most people <u>admire</u> a mud puddle?

3. Do police cars and fire trucks have sirens that <u>chime</u>?

4. Does a dictionary <u>define</u> words?

## Write to the Point

Many wildlife parks have signs near the animals' living areas. The signs give interesting facts about the animals. Choose an animal that you like. Then make a sign telling about the animal. Use spelling words from this lesson in your sign.

**Challenge** Use one or more of the Challenge Words in your sign.

## Proofreading

Use the marks to show the errors in the sentences below. Write the four misspelled words correctly in the blanks.

| | |
|---|---|
| ◯ | word is misspelled |
| ═ | letter should be capitalized |
| ꟼ | take out word |

1. the lien opened his mouth.

2. From deep insid came a roar.

3. The sound traveled for for many mials.

4. his voice wasn't tiny like myn.

1. _____

2. _____

3. _____

4. _____

# Lesson 16 Words with /ī/

**Listen for /ī/ as you say each word.**

Friday

kind

child

mind

behind

high

right

light

night

by

cry

sky

try

why

fly

buy

1. Which two words have two syllables?

_____  _____

2. Which two words sound exactly the same but are not spelled the same?

_____  _____

3. Which three words have the last four letters of sight? _____

_____  _____

4. Write the word that begins and ends with the letter h. _____

5. Write three words that end with the last three letters of find. _____

_____  _____

6. Write six words that spell /ī/ with the letter y.

_____  _____

_____  _____

_____  _____

7. Which word begins with the letters ch?

_____

8. Which word always begins with a capital letter?

# Checkpoint

Write a spelling word for each clue.
Then use the Checkpoint Study Plan on page 224.

1. The opposite of mean is ——.

2. The time between sunset and sunrise is ——.

3. Tears come out of your eyes when you ——.

4. To pay money for something is to ——.

5. If you follow someone, you are ——.

6. The last day of school each week is ——.

7. The part of you that thinks is your ——.

8. Rabbits hop, and birds ——.

9. The opposite of low is ——.

10. "To make an effort" means to ——.

11. You ask what, when, where, and ——.

12. "Beside" or "near to" means ——.

13. The sun gives us heat and ——.

14. The opposite of left is ——.

15. A boy or a girl is a ——.

16. This mystery word comes from the Old English
word *skie. Skie* meant cloud. *Skie* also meant the
place where you see clouds. That's what the
word means today. Guess the word. ——

Use each word once to complete this story.

# Living Room Circus

Last _____ my family and I were

going to the circus. But I got sick.

Mom made a bed for me on the couch. Then

she opened the door to let Tinker in.

Tinker is our cat. He sleeps all day in the warm

_____ of the sun. Every _____

he gets to play. I always _____ to talk Mom

and Dad into letting me stay up all night. If a cat

can, _____ can't I? They don't agree.

Well, that day, Tinker dropped a fat pigeon

_____ my dad's feet.

"Oh, no," Mom cried. "How could you bring

that in the house?"

Mom thinks you can talk to Tinker like you can

talk to a _____ . She gets very angry

when Tinker acts like a cat. Mom doesn't allow

that _____ of behavior from anyone!

Just then, the bird fluttered its wings. It wasn't dead. It began to _____ around the room. It flew _____ up to the ceiling.

Tinker saw the pigeon and hid _____ the couch. He jumped out as the bird whizzed by.

Mom opened the door. Tinker chased the pigeon. Dad chased Tinker. My baby brother began to _____. And I began to laugh. You couldn't _____ a ticket to a better show.

Finally, the bird flew out the door. Tinker was _____ behind it. But the pigeon flew high into the _____.

I was glad that the bird was safe. And I didn't _____ that I was sick. I got to see a circus after all!

89

Friday
kind
child
mind
behind
high
right
light
night
by
cry
sky
try
why
fly
buy

# Alphabetical Order

Many words begin with the same letter. To put these words in alphabetical order, look at the second letter of each word. Begin your list with the word in which the second letter comes first in the alphabet.

⭐ Look at the two words below.

**s<u>k</u>y**　　　**s<u>t</u>ory**

1. These words both start with the letter <u>s</u>. To put them in

   alphabetical order, look at the _____ letter.

2. The second letter in <u>sk</u>y is ____ .

3. The second letter in <u>st</u>ory is ____ .

4. In the alphabet, <u>k</u> comes before <u>t</u>, so the word

   _____ comes before the word _____ .

⭐ In each list below, the words begin with the same letter. Look at the second letter of each word. Then write the words in alphabetical order.

5. **buy　　behind　　by**　　　　6. **cry　　child　　cart**

   _____　　　　　　　_____

   _____　　　　　　　_____

7. **fly　　Friday　　finish**　　　　8. **light　　late　　llama**

   _____　　　　　　　_____

# WORDS AT WORK

## Challenge Yourself

**designer    glider    cycle    skyline**

Decide which Challenge Word fits each clue. Check your Spelling Dictionary to see if you were right. Then write sentences showing that you understand the meaning of each Challenge Word.

1. It has wings but is not a bird.

2. A big city has one of these.

3. If you ride something with two wheels, you have one of these.

4. This is a person who makes drawings and plans.

## Write to the Point

In the story "Living Room Circus," the word <u>circus</u> means "an exciting time." Write a paragraph about an exciting time. The paragraph can be about you or someone else. Use spelling words from this lesson in your paragraph.

**Challenge** Use one or more of the Challenge Words in your paragraph.

## Proofreading

Use the marks to show the errors in the sentences below. Write the four misspelled words correctly in the blanks.

| | |
|---|---|
| ◯ | word is misspelled |
| ⊙ | period is missing |
| ⌇ | take out word |

1. Tinker is the kind of cat that will trie anything

2. On Friday he put my cap bahind the couch

3. He has a a miend of his own.

4. I don't know whiy we keep that kind of pet.

1. _____

2. _____

3. _____

4. _____

91

# Lesson 17 Adding ed and ing

**Say each word.**

wished

asked

dreamed

rained

handed

painted

filled

subtracted

thanked

waited


reading

sleeping

meeting

laughing

guessing

ending

**Complete the word equations.**

1. fill    +   ed   = _____

2. ask    +   ed   = _____

3. rain    +   ed   = _____

4. wait    +   ed   = _____

5. wish    +   ed   = _____

6. hand    +   ed   = _____

7. paint    +   ed   = _____

8. thank    +   ed   = _____

9. dream    +   ed   = _____

10. subtract   +   ed   = _____

11. end    +   ing   = _____

12. read    +   ing   = _____

13. meet    +   ing   = _____

14. sleep    +   ing   = _____

15. laugh    +   ing   = _____

16. guess    +   ing   = _____

**Answer this question.**

17. In which three words do the letters _ed_ spell /t/?

_____

92

# Checkpoint

Write a spelling word for each clue.
Then use the Checkpoint Study Plan on page 224.

1. The last part of a story is the ____.

2. Are you right-handed or left-____.

3. "Made a picture with paints" means ____.

4. If you made a wish, you ____.

5. "Went to sleep and had a dream" means ____.

6. The opposite of crying is ____.

7. When people get together to talk, it's a ____.

8. Giving an answer you're not sure about is ____.

9. "Stayed until someone came" means ____.

10. When you're not awake, you're ____.

11. "Put a question to someone" means ____.

12. If water fell from the sky, then it ____.

13. "Told someone thank you" means ____.

14. The opposite of emptied is ____.

15. Libraries have books for ____.

16. This mystery word means to take away or to make less. It comes from two Latin words. The words are *sub* and *trahere*. *Sub* meant below or away. *Trahere* meant to pull. *Subtrahere* meant to pull away. Can you guess the word made from *subtrahere* + <u>ed</u>? ____

93

# THE PLAYOFFS

When I left hockey practice last night, it was still raining. It had _____ all day.

I _____ for my dad to pick me up. Then I remembered that Mom and Dad were at a _____ with my teachers. So I walked over to school to wait.

I tried not to think about the homework that I hadn't done yet. I had extra problems to do because I added numbers on our last test when I should have _____ them. Oh, how I _____ that I had done my math before practice. Then I would have been finished.

At school I ran into Ms. Ford, the art teacher. She was showing the parents pictures that students had _____. Mr. Chan, the librarian, was also at school. I _____ if I could wait in the library. He said yes. Then he _____ me a book that he was sure I would like. I _____ him and sat at a table.

94

The book was about the hockey goalie, Gerry Cheevers. It was _____ with pictures. I started _____. The book was great. I could hardly wait to read the _____.

The next thing I knew, I was on the floor, swinging my arms and yelling. My parents were there. They were _____ at me. I shook my head and blinked. "Was I _____?" I asked.

"I'm only _____," Dad said, "but I would say you _____ you were a hockey player. The way you were swinging your arms around, I'm glad I wasn't the other guy!"

I grinned. Too bad it was just a dream.

95

wished
asked
dreamed
rained
handed
painted
filled
subtracted
thanked
waited
reading
sleeping
meeting
laughing
guessing
ending

# Exclamation Points

Use an exclamation point (!) at the end of a sentence that shows strong feeling or surprise.

*Open that door!*
*I'm so happy you're here!*

⭐ Write each sentence below. Put an exclamation point, a period, or a question mark at the end of each sentence.

1. Betsy asked, "Who painted this picture   "

2. She was guessing that Paul had done it

3. She found Paul sleeping

4. Betsy shouted, "Boo   "

5. Paul jumped up fast

6. "Oh, Betsy   " he yelled. "Now I'll never know the ending of my dream   "

7. Then they both started laughing

# WORDS AT WORK

## Challenge Yourself

fulfilling      faltering
     consented      governed

What do you think each underlined Challenge Word means? Check your Spelling Dictionary to see if you are right. Then write sentences showing that you understand the meaning of each Challenge Word.

1. He is <u>fulfilling</u> his promise.

2. A beginning skater may make <u>faltering</u> movements on the ice.

3. Mom <u>consented</u> to let us play.

4. The President <u>governed</u> the country for four years.

## Write to the Point

You dream almost every time you sleep. Dreams can take you on great adventures. Sometimes dreams are happy. Other times they're silly. Write a paragraph about a dream you've had. Use spelling words from this lesson in your paragraph.

**Challenge** Use one or more of the Challenge Words in your paragraph.

## Proofreading

Use the marks to show the errors in the sentences below. Write the four misspelled words correctly in the blanks.

| | |
|---|---|
| ◯ | word is misspelled |
| ⊙ | period is missing |
| ＝ | letter should be capitalized |

1. last night I dreamd about my coach, Mr. Flowers.

2. The team was in a meating.

3. Everyone was handid a book and was asked to read it

4. I woke up before the endin.

1. _____

2. _____

3. _____

4. _____

# Lesson 18 Words in Review

**A.** won

    lovely

    hundred

**B.** kick

    river

    pretty

    build

    been

**C.** shine

    tiny

    lion

    eyes

**D.** behind

    high

    sky

    buy

★ Use a piece of paper for the starred activities.

1. In Lesson 13 you studied two ways to spell /ŭ/: **o, u.** Write the words in list A.

2. In Lesson 14 you studied four ways to spell /ĭ/: **i, e, ui, ee.** Write the words in list B.

★3. Now write the review words in lists A and B. Look them up in the Spelling Dictionary and write the sound spelling next to each word.

4. In Lesson 15 you studied three ways to spell /ī/: **i_e, i, eye.** Write the words in list C.

5. In Lesson 16 you studied three more ways to spell /ī/: **i, y, uy.** Write the words in list D.

★6. Now write a sentence for each review word in lists C and D.

★7. Write sentences for the words in A and B.

★8. Write the review words from lists C and D in alphabetical order.

# A Friendly Letter

Everyone likes to get letters from friends and family members. People write friendly letters to tell about themselves, their thoughts, and their feelings. Here is the greeting and body of Elena's letter to her friend Gwen.

> **Dear Gwen,**
>
> **Our new house is great! I can see the park from my bedroom window. Sometimes I walk there with Pooch. He loves to chase the birds. When they fly away, he barks and runs in circles.**
> **A girl named Lily lives next door. She's nice, but I really miss you.**

To write her letter, Elena followed the steps in the writing process. She began by deciding to whom she would write. Then she did a **Prewriting** activity using a list. The list helped her decide what to tell Gwen in the letter. Part of Elena's list is shown here. Study what she did.

New House
can see park
Pooch chases birds
park closed Monday

New Friend
Lily

**It's Your Turn**

Get ready to write your own friendly letter. Tell about a special event or about your thoughts and feelings. After you have decided to whom you will write, make a list of things you want to say. Then follow the other steps in the writing process—**Writing, Revising, Proofreading,** and **Publishing**.

# Lesson 19 Words with /ŏ/

**Listen for /ŏ/ as you say each word.**

sorry

socks

clock

bottom

block

problem

jog

o'clock

October

forgot

shop

bottle

body


wash

what

was

1. In which four words do the letters <u>ck</u> spell /k/?

_____     _____

_____     _____

2. Which three words have double consonants?

rr _____     tt _____

tt _____

3. Which two words have the letters <u>sh</u>?

_____     _____

4. Write two words that have only three letters.

_____     _____

5. In which word does the letter <u>s</u> spell /z/?

_____

6. Which word is always spelled with a capital letter? _____

7. Write a word that begins with /hw/.

_____

8. Write two words that end with the vowel /ē/.

_____     _____

9. Which word begins with the letter <u>p</u> and has two syllables? _____

10. Which word begins with the letter <u>f</u> and has two syllables? _____

# Checkpoint

Write a spelling word for each clue.
Then use the Checkpoint Study Plan on page 224.

1. When you buy food, you ——.

2. To clean with water and soap is to ——.

3. From your head to your feet is your ——.

4. To run slowly is to ——.

5. If you're sad you did something, you're ——.

6. Over your feet and under your shoes are ——.

7. From one street corner to another is one ——.

8. Today I am, yesterday I ——.

9. "Which thing" means ——.

10. The opposite of remembered is ——.

11. A container that holds liquids is a ——.

12. The month before November is ——.

13. A word for "of the clock" is ——.

14. The lowest part of anything is the ——.

15. A hard question to answer is a ——.

16. This mystery word names an instrument that
    tells the time of day. The word comes from the
    Old French word *cloque*. *Cloque* meant bell.
    These instruments used to be made with bells.
    The bells rang when a new hour arrived. Today
    only a few of these instruments have bells. Can
    you guess the mystery word? ——

# Alphabetical Order

⭐ Look at these sample entry words from a dictionary:

*block    bottle    butter*

**1.** What is the same about the words? _____

Words that begin with the same letter are put into alphabetical order by using the second letter.

**b**l**ock      b**o**ttle          b**u**tter**

. . . k  l  m  n  o  p  q  r  s  t  u  v . . .

⭐ Look at the second letter of each word. Then write each group of words in alphabetical order.

**2. bottle  block  bank  butter**

_____

_____

_____

**3. shop  salt  socks  stack**

_____

_____

_____

**4. was  wonder  west  what**

_____

_____

_____

**5. problem  paint  plaster  pound**

_____

_____

_____

**6. October    orange    often    other**

_____

_____

_____

# WORDS AT WORK

## Challenge Yourself

**deposit apologize waffle comment**

What do you think each underlined Challenge Word means? Check your Spelling Dictionary to see if you are right. Then write sentences showing that you understand the meaning of each Challenge Word.

1. Marie decided to <u>deposit</u> a note in a bottle.

2. You should <u>apologize</u> when you hurt someone's feelings.

3. A hot <u>waffle</u> would taste good for breakfast.

4. What <u>comment</u> did his father make about his grades?

## Write to the Point

Have you ever had a problem with a friend? Perhaps your friend had a habit that bothered you. What did you do to make things better? Write a paragraph describing the problem and tell what you did. Use spelling words from this lesson in your paragraph.

**Challenge** Use one or more of the Challenge Words in your paragraph.

## Proofreading

Use the marks to show the errors in the paragraph below. Write the four misspelled words correctly in the blanks.

⬭ word is misspelled

⊙ period is missing

↶ take out word

Len checked the clok. It was time for for his jogg around the block There was one problum. He could not find his sox and water bottle.

1. _____

2. _____

3. _____

4. _____

105

# Lesson 20 Words with /ō/

**Listen for /ō/ as you say each word.**

hope

alone

whole

hole

close

joke

wrote

slow

know

yellow

blow

snow

show

goes

toe

November

1. Which two words sound exactly alike but are not spelled alike?

_____  _____

2. Which word begins with the letter g?

_____

3. Write six words that end with the letter w but not the sound /w/.

_____  _____

_____  _____

_____  _____

4. Write two words that begin with the letter w but not the sound /w/.

_____  _____

5. Write three words that have more than one syllable. _____

_____  _____

6. Which word begins with the letter j?

_____

7. Which word begins with /k/? _____

8. Which word ends with the last two letters of woe? _____

9. Which word ends with /p/? _____

# Checkpoint

Write a spelling word for each clue.
Then use the Checkpoint Study Plan on page 224.

1. The color of the sun is ——.

2. Another word for play or program is ——.

3. The month before December is ——.

4. When you're sure about something, you ——.

5. Your foot has a big ——.

6. When there's no one else around, you are ——.

7. In summer we get rain, in winter we get ——.

8. To wish for something is to ——.

9. All the pieces together make a ——.

10. The opposite of fast is ——.

11. To make a candle go out, you ——.

12. A word for moves along is ——.

13. With your shovel you dig a ——.

14. The opposite of far away is ——.

15. The past tense of write is ——.

16. This mystery word comes from the Latin word *jocus*. Both the English and the French borrowed the word *jocus* and changed it. The French changed it to *jugleor*, which means juggler. A juggler is a person who does funny things. The English changed *jocus* to the mystery word. The mystery word means a funny story. Can you guess it? ——

Use each word once to complete this story.

# WHAT ARE FRIENDS FOR?

Peter _____ a note to Jacob. Peter said he wanted to be _____. Jacob knew Peter was sad because his dog had run away. He decided to go see Peter anyway.

Jacob had a plan. He would tell a funny _____. He would make Peter laugh if it took the _____ day to do it.

"Why did the boy _____ the door and leave his father out in the month of _____?" Jacob asked.

Peter didn't answer. He stared at his dog's picture. "Because he wanted cold pop." Jacob laughed. Peter didn't even smile.

Jacob asked, "What kind of nail hurts when you hit it?" Peter didn't look up.

"A _____ nail." Jacob smiled. Peter didn't.

Jacob tried again. "What comes after a snowstorm?" Peter didn't answer. Jacob said, "_____ shovels. Here is another one. What _____ away when you fill it up?"

"I wish <u>you</u> would go away," Peter said.

108

Jacob was hurt. He tried not to _____

it. He knew Peter was hurting, too. So he said, "A

_____. What did the north wind say to the

west wind?"

"I don't _____," said Peter.

Jacob told him the answer anyway. "It's time to

_____."

"I _____ you don't have any more

awful jokes," Peter said.

Jacob gave up. He ran out the door. Peter

yelled, "Jacob, _____ down."

Jacob slipped on a banana peel. He flew up in

the air and landed in a pile of bright red and

_____ leaves. All Peter could see

was Jacob's nose. Peter laughed and laughed.

Peter wiped his eyes and said, "Thanks for

making me laugh."

Jacob smiled and said, "That's what friends are

for, Peter."

109

hope
alone
whole
hole
close
joke
wrote
slow
know
yellow
blow
snow
show
goes
toe
November

# Verbs

A verb is a word that expresses action.

*jumped    laughed    sat    sang*

⭐Write the verb in each group of words below.

1. wrote    whole    house

2. November    road    hope

3. ago    goes    hello

4. yellow    most    know

⭐Unscramble the spelling words as you write each sentence below. Then circle the verbs.

5. John hurt his oet.

6. Please wosh me your new sneakers.

7. nows fell all night long.

8. We ate the lewoh pizza.

9. Krista bought a loweyl skateboard.

10. They dug a lohe in the yard.

110

## Challenge Yourself

**adobe  console  rodent  dome**

Decide which Challenge Word fits each clue. Check your Spelling Dictionary to see if you were right. Then write sentences showing that you understand the meaning of each Challenge Word.

1. The roof of some buildings is one of these.

2. A mouse is this kind of animal.

3. Some homes in the Southwest are made of this.

4. You might do this to a friend who is sad.

## Write to the Point

Jacob told Peter jokes and riddles to make him laugh. They didn't work. Write a joke or riddle that will make Jacob laugh. You may rewrite one that you heard before or make up a new one of your own. Use spelling words from this lesson in your joke.

**Challenge** Use one or more of the Challenge Words in your joke.

## Proofreading

Use the marks to show the errors in the paragraph below. Write the four misspelled words correctly in the blanks.

| | |
|---|---|
| ⬭ | word is misspelled |
| ⊙ | period is missing |
| ☰ | letter should be capitalized |

it's November, and snoe is

falling. My cat rita has been gone

for a hole day. I feel so aloan. I

hoppe she comes back home soon

1. _____

2. _____

3. _____

4. _____

# Lesson 21  Words with /ō/

Listen for /ō/ as you say each word.

both

ago

almost

hold

comb

gold

hello

open

most

over


road

toast

loaf

boat

cocoa

coat

1. Write two words that begin with the letter o.

_____    _____

2. Write the word in which you see the letter b but don't hear /b/. _____

3. In which two-syllable word are both syllables pronounced /kō/? _____

4. Write three words that end with the letters st.

_____    _____

_____

5. Which three words end with a vowel?

_____    _____

_____

6. Write the two words that end with the letters ld.

_____    _____

7. Write a word that ends with the letters th.

_____

8. Write two words that end with the last three letters of goat.

_____    _____

9. Write six words in which the letters oa spell /ō/.

_____    _____

_____    _____

# Checkpoint

Write a spelling word for each clue.
Then use the Checkpoint Study Plan on page 224.

1. To keep something in your hand is to ——.

2. Bread that is baked in one big pan is a ——.

3. Something you wear to keep warm in is a ——.

4. When you meet someone, you say ——.

5. Arrange your hair with a brush and a ——.

6. A yellow metal used to make rings is ——.

7. "Nearly, but not quite" means ——.

8. You put butter, jam, or jelly on ——.

9. The opposite of closed is ——.

10. Something to sail in is a ——.

11. The opposite of under is ——.

12. Another word for street is ——.

13. "Not one but two" means ——.

14. The opposite of least is ——.

15. "In the past" means ——.

16. Sometimes a new word comes from misspelling an old word. This mystery word names a food we often add to milk. The food comes from the beans of a tree. The tree is called the *cacao* tree. At first this food was called *cacao*. But many people misspelled *cacao*. Can you guess the word? ——

Use each word once to complete this story.

# Fool's Paradise

Last summer we went to a lake that had an island in the middle of it. The island was tiny. It was called Fool's Paradise. There was a legend about the island. Many years _____ a treasure was buried there. The treasure was never found.

My sister Devon was excited about the legend. One day she packed a _____ of bread and some cheese. Then she got in a _____ and rowed to the island. Devon was going to comb every inch of it until she found the treasure.

Devon had been gone _____ three hours when a storm came up. Mom and Dad _____ were worried. So was I. Devon can take care of herself _____ of the time. But this was the worst storm I had ever seen.

Just then, Devon came running down the _____ to our cabin. "_____!" she yelled, as she came inside, dripping water all _____ everything.

"Change those wet clothes and _____ your hair," Dad said.

114

I said I would make some _____
and _____ .

"Wait," said Devon. "The storm blew over a tree on the island. I found something buried under it." She reached into her _____ pockets. "Close your eyes and _____ out your hands." We thought she was crazy. But we did it. Devon put rocks into our hands.

"Okay," she said, "_____ your eyes."

The rocks looked just like _____ . Then Mother said, "Oh, Devon. You've fallen for an old trick. That's only fool's gold."

Devon hadn't found a treasure. She had only found rocks that looked like gold. But now we know why the island is called Fool's Paradise.

both
ago
almost
hold
comb
gold
hello
open
most
over
road
toast
loaf
boat
cocoa
coat

# Synonyms

Words that have the same meaning, or almost the same meaning, are called <u>synonyms</u>.

*Hello    Howdy    Welcome    Hi*

★ Find a synonym from the spelling list for each word in the crossword puzzle. Then write the synonym clues for the puzzle.

ACROSS

3. _____

4. _____

6. _____

7. _____

DOWN

1. _____

2. _____

3. _____

5. _____

6. _____

Hooray! You finished. Here's a synonym toast for you.

**Good luck!    CONGRATULATIONS!    Salud!    Prosit!**

(Spanish)    (German)

116

## Challenge Yourself

**coax    solo    rodeo    patrol**

Use your Spelling Dictionary to answer these questions. Then write sentences showing that you understand the meaning of each Challenge Word.

1. Would a person <u>coax</u> cereal into a bowl?

2. Was Devon's trip to the island a <u>solo</u> trip?

3. Did Devon find a <u>rodeo</u> in the middle of the lake?

4. Was Devon hoping to find a <u>patrol</u> on the island?

## Write to the Point

Devon was excited about the legend of the buried treasure. Write a paragraph about a buried treasure you would like to find. What kind of treasure would it be? Where do you think you might find it? Use spelling words from this lesson in your paragraph.

**Challenge** Use one or more of the Challenge Words in your paragraph.

## Proofreading

Use the marks to show the errors in the paragraph below. Write the four misspelled words correctly in the blanks.

| ◯ | word is misspelled |
| ≡ | letter should be capitalized |
| ✋ | take out word |

Don't go in a small open bote in a storm. strong winds can blow it ovre. you might not be able to to holde on. Do moast people know this?

1. _____

2. _____

3. _____

4. _____

# Lesson 22 Words with /o͝o/

Listen for /o͝o/ as you say each word.

book

cookies

took

stood

wood

poor

foot

cook

shook

put

full

pull

sure

should

could

would

1. Which two words sound exactly alike but are not spelled alike?

_____ _____

2. Write three words in which you see the letter l but don't hear /l/.

_____

_____

3. In which word does the letter s spell /sh/?

_____

4. Write four words that end with the last three letters of look.

_____ _____

_____ _____

5. In which word do you hear two syllables?

_____

6. Write three words that begin with the letter p.

_____ _____

_____

7. Which two words end with the last three letters of good?

_____

8. Write two words that begin with the letter f.

_____

# Checkpoint

Write a spelling word for each clue.
Then use the Checkpoint Study Plan on page 224.

1. We baked cakes, pies, and ____.

2. If you know for certain, you know for ____.

3. "To place" means to ____.

4. In a game of tug of war, take a rope and ____.

5. When you got up on your feet, you ____.

6. When you can't hold any more, you're ____.

7. "Ought to" means ____.

8. The opposite of rich is ____.

9. The past tense of shake is ____.

10. Today I can, yesterday I ____.

11. The past tense of take is ____.

12. Today I will, yesterday I ____.

13. To heat food on a stove is to ____.

14. You wear your shoe on your ____.

15. The trunk of a tree is made of ____.

16. Did you ever wonder what people wrote on
    before paper was invented? In England, people
    peeled bark off beech trees. The Old English
    word for beech was *bok*. When paper was
    invented, people stopped writing on bark.
    Instead, they tied papers together and wrote on
    them. They called this thing by a name that
    comes from the word *bok*. Can you guess the
    mystery word? ____

Use each word once to complete this story.

# THE LITTLE MOUSE

Morris, the mouse, peeked over the top of

the _____ pile. The lion was asleep.

Then he saw the chocolate _____

beside the lion's left _____ .

Morris wondered if he _____ try

to get one of the cookies. The little mouse was very

hungry. He decided to take the chance.

Morris tiptoed over to the lion. He reached out

to _____ the cookies toward him. Whack!

The lion _____ his big foot down on the little

mouse. The lion _____ up and roared.

Morris was scared. He _____ like a leaf.

Morris thought fast. He said, "Mr. Lion, I'm just

a _____ little mouse. You would have to

build a fire to _____ me. Are you really

_____ I would be worth the trouble?"

The lion thought about it. He was still very

_____ from his last meal. So the lion told

the mouse to hurry away before he changed his

mind. Morris thanked him and was gone.

120

The next day, two hunters were looking for big game. They had read in a _____ that there were lots of lions in this country. The hunters saw the sleeping lion. They _____ out a net and threw it over him. There was nothing the lion _____ do except yell for help.

Morris heard the lion's cry. He looked until he found the lion. He said he _____ try to help. The lion said, "You are too small to help."

Morris didn't answer. He began to nibble on the net with his sharp teeth. Soon the little mouse had made a big hole. The lion was free.

That is how the lion learned that good things often come in small packages.

121

book
cookies
took
stood
wood
poor
foot
cook
shook
put
full
pull
sure
should
could
would

# Capitals

The names of cities and states always begin with a capital letter.

*New York City is the largest city in this country.*
*Phoenix is the capital of Arizona.*

★Unscramble the spelling words as you write each sentence. Put capital letters where they belong.

1. many dowo products come from maine.

_____

2. you can put your otfo in four states at once: new mexico, utah, colorado, and arizona. _____

_____

_____

3. the rues winner for the largest state is alaska.

_____

_____

4. everyone dosluh visit chicago, illinois.

_____

5. dowlu you like to go to new orleans?

_____

6. san francisco ohsko during an earthquake.

_____

_____

7. i live in (fill in your town or city), (fill in your state).

_____

8. my state capital is (fill in name).

_____

## Challenge Yourself

**bureau  gourmet  assure  endure**

What do you think each underlined Challenge Word means? Check your Spelling Dictionary to see if you are right. Then write sentences showing that you understand the meaning of each Challenge Word.

1. A mouse was living in my bureau drawer.

2. It nibbled on the gourmet cheese Mom bought.

3. Can you assure me it has gone and won't come back?

4. I could not endure one more night of its noisy squeaks.

## Write to the Point

The lion must have been surprised that a mouse had saved his life. He probably thanked the mouse. Write a thank-you note to a person who has done something to help you. Describe what happened and why you are happy the person helped you. Use spelling words from this lesson in your note.

**Challenge** Use one or more of the Challenge Words in your note.

## Proofreading

Use the marks to show the errors in the paragraph below. Write the four misspelled words correctly in the blanks.

Mom putt a dish of cookies on the table  They shur looked good, and I I almost took one. But Mom shuk her head  Next time I wood ask first.

| | |
|---|---|
| ◯ | word is misspelled |
| ⊙ | period is missing |
| ✍ | take out word |

1. _____

2. _____

3. _____

4. _____

123

# Lesson 23 Adding ed and ing

**Say each word.**

closed

hoped

liked

sneezed

pleased


stopped

jogged

dropped


taking

smiling

driving

shining


beginning

hopping

dropping

shopping

**Complete the word equations.**

1. like     − e + ed = _____

2. hope    − e + ed = _____

3. close    − e + ed = _____

4. please   − e + ed = _____

5. sneeze − e + ed = _____


6. take     − e + ing = _____

7. drive    − e + ing = _____

8. smile    − e + ing = _____

9. shine    − e + ing = _____


10. jog     + g + ed = _____

11. stop    + p + ed = _____

12. drop    + p + ed = _____


13. hop     + p + ing = _____

14. drop    + p + ing = _____

15. shop    + p + ing = _____

16. begin + n + ing = _____

**Answer this question.**

17. In which four words do the letters <u>ed</u> spell /t/?

_____

_____

# Checkpoint

Write a spelling word for each clue.
Then use the Checkpoint Study Plan on page 224.

1. The start is the ——.

2. Someone who had a cold coughed and ——.

3. If you wished for something, you ——.

4. "Letting something fall" means ——.

5. When the sun is bright, the sun is ——.

6. Another word for grinning is ——.

7. The opposite of started is ——.

8. Another word for happy is ——.

9. "Let fall" means ——.

10. Another word for enjoyed is ——.

11. The opposite of giving is ——.

12. Making a car go is ——.

13. The opposite of open is ——.

14. Kangaroos are always ——.

15. "Ran slowly" means ——.

16. Long ago in England there were places called
    *schoppes.* A *schoppe* was a booth in a marketplace.
    People sold things there. There is a verb that
    means to buy things in a *schoppe.* It comes from
    the word *schoppe* itself. This verb plus <u>ing</u> makes
    the mystery word. Can you guess it? ——

# SUMMER DAYS

Tim and his brother Lester _____

summer vacation. But it was already the

_____ of August. They

wanted something new to do.

The sun was _____

brightly. It was a hot day. The boys spent the

morning looking for something to do. They had

_____ to find a job.

By one o'clock they had given up. Nobody

needed their help.

Tim and Lester were sitting on the front steps of

their house when their dad opened the door. He

was _____ into town. Dad was

_____ the car to be fixed and

was going _____ for food.

Dad asked, "Do you want to come along?" The

boys shook their heads no. Dad understood the

boys wanted to be alone.

He said, "Just keep looking. You can't expect a job to fall out of the sky." He _____ the door and left.

Tim started _____ up and down. "Look at the field, Lester. It's raining paper!"

Sure enough, paper was _____ out of a helicopter.

At first the boys _____ toward the field. But as they got closer, they ran.

As the papers _____ to the ground, Lester caught one. He started to laugh. He laughed so hard he started to sneeze. Lester always _____ when he laughed. Tim started laughing, too. The paper said:

---

Dirty Dan's Clean-up Crew

We will be _____ to clean up anything. If you have a mess, just call 555-5555.

P.S.   Need a job? We'll pay 10¢ for every 100 pieces of paper you pick up.

Dirty Dan

---

Finally, Lester and Tim _____ laughing. Now they were _____ from ear to ear. They had found jobs at last.

127

closed
hoped
liked
sneezed
pleased
stopped
jogged
dropped
taking
smiling
driving
shining
beginning
hopping
dropping
shopping

# Commas

To make it easy to read a date, put a comma between the day and the year because they are different numbers.

*July 4, 1776*

⭐ Write the dates below. Put in the commas.

1. March 23    1976 _____

2. December 27    1972 _____

3. Today's month, day, and year are _____ .

4. I was born on _____ .

⭐ Write the sentences below. Use one of these spelling words to finish each sentence. Put commas where they belong.

**jogged    closed**
**dropped   hoped**

5. School ___ for vacation on June 23    1980.

_____

6. On January 25    1978, Lisa's mom ___ in a six-mile race.

_____

_____

7. Old friends ___ in to visit us on February 4    1980.

_____

_____

8. Jana ___ the party would be on May 17    1982.

_____

# WORDS AT WORK

## Challenge Yourself

jabbing            crinkled
      estimated            stunned

What do you think each underlined
Challenge Word means? Check your
Spelling Dictionary to see if you are
right. Then write sentences showing
that you understand the meaning of
each Challenge Word.

1.  I wasn't jabbing it with a stick.

2.  Straighten the crinkled paper.

3.  We estimated that we picked up
    about 500 pieces of paper.

4.  Its huge size stunned me!

## Write to the Point

What message would you like to
send by helicopter? Would you
look for a job or spread some good
news? Write your message on
pieces of paper. Use spelling words
from this lesson in your message.

**Challenge** Use one or more of the
Challenge Words in your message.

## Proofreading

Use the marks to show the errors
in the paragraph below. Write the
four misspelled words correctly in
the blanks.

    once I saved cans that people had

dropped. I joged to the store and got

money for them  I was so pleasd. I

likd having my own money  Later I

went shoping in chicago.

| | |
|---|---|
| ◯ | word is misspelled |
| ⊙ | period is missing |
| ≡ | letter should be capitalized |

1. _____

2. _____

3. _____

4. _____

129

# Lesson 24 Words in Review

**A.** socks

bottom

wash

**B.** wrote

know

yellow

goes

November

**C.** comb

hello

road

cocoa

**D.** cookies

shook

sure

should

★ Use a piece of paper for the starred activities.

1. In Lesson 19 you studied two ways to spell /ŏ/: **o, a.** Write the words in list A.

2. In Lesson 20 you studied four ways to spell /ō/: **o_e, ow, oe, o.** Write the words in list B.

★ 3. Now write a sentence for each review word in lists A and B.

4. In Lesson 21 you studied two ways to spell /ō/: **o, oa.** Write the words in list C.

5. In Lesson 22 you studied three ways to spell /o͝o/: **oo, u, ou.** Write the words in list D.

★ 6. Now write the review words in lists C and D. Look up each word in the Spelling Dictionary and write the guide words at the top of the page for each word.

★ 7. Now write the words in lists A and B in alphabetical order.

# Writer's Workshop

## A Description

A description tells about a person, a place, or a thing. The writer uses details that appeal to a reader's sense of sight, hearing, smell, touch, and taste. Here is part of Ben's description of a baseball game.

### The Game

My granddad took me to my first baseball game last summer. It was a perfect day. The sun was bright and yellow. I could smell the green, grassy field. A huge American flag in right field waved in the gentle breeze. Our seats were right behind home plate. I could hear the thump of the ball in the catcher's mitt. I could see the players' frowns when the umpire called, "You're out!"

To write his description, Ben followed the steps in the writing process. He began with a **Prewriting** activity using a senses web. There he listed details about his topic. The web helped him decide which sense words to include in his description. Part of Ben's senses web is shown here. Study what Ben did.

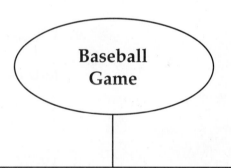

Baseball Game

**Hearing**
thump of ball in catcher's mitt
umpire's call
crowd cheering

**It's Your Turn**

Get ready to write your own description. It can be about a place, a person, or anything you can picture clearly in your mind. After you have decided what to describe, make a senses web. Then follow the other steps in the writing process—**Writing**, **Revising**, **Proofreading**, and **Publishing**.

# Lesson 25 /ōō/ and /yōō/

Listen for /ōō/ or /yōō/ as you say each word.

noon

school

too

tooth

blue

true

Tuesday

who

move

two

news

knew

June

July

★

few

used

1. Write the five words in which you see the letter <u>w</u> but don't hear /w/. _____

_____

2. Which three words are always spelled with a capital letter? _____

_____

3. Which four words have double vowels?

_____

_____

4. Which two words end with the last two letters of <u>glue</u>?

_____

5. Write three words that have the letters <u>ew</u>.

_____

_____

6. Write three words in which you hear /z/ but don't see the letter <u>z</u>. _____

_____

7. Which word ends with the sound /v/?

_____

132

# Checkpoint

Write a spelling word for each clue.
Then use the Checkpoint Study Plan on page 224.

1. The opposite of false is ____.

2. The month that comes before August is ____.

3. In newspapers you can read the ____.

4. The dentist pulled her baby ____.

5. One plus one is ____.

6. To go from one place to another is to ____.

7. A place where people go to learn is a ____.

8. The opposite of many is ____.

9. The time of day for eating lunch is ____.

10. Another word for also is ____.

11. Something that is useful can be ____.

12. The month after May is ____.

13. The color of the sky is ____.

14. "What person" means ____.

15. Today I know, yesterday I ____.

16. Have you ever heard of the Vikings? They were
people from northern Europe. The Vikings gave
us our mystery word. The mystery word comes
from the word *Tiwdaeg*. *Tiw* was the Old
English name for the Viking war god. *Daeg*
meant day. Can you guess which modern
word comes from *Tiwdaeg*? ____

# Pronunciation

Words are not always pronounced the way they are spelled. The dictionary shows us how to say a word. The way a word is said is called its <u>pronunciation</u>. In a dictionary, the pronunciation is written as a sound spelling after the entry word.

**Entry Word** →

> **school** | skōol | —*noun, plural* **schools**
> A place of teaching and learning: *We learned about Japan in school.*

**Pronunciation Sound Spelling**

The dictionary uses letters and symbols to write a sound spelling. These letters and symbols can be found in the <u>pronunciation key</u>.

| | | | | | |
|---|---|---|---|---|---|
| /ă/ | pat | /ŏ/ | pot | /ŭ/ | cut |
| /ā/ | pay | /ō/ | toe | /û/ | urge |
| /â/ | care | /ô/ | paw, | /zh/ | vision |
| /ä/ | father | | for | /ə/ | about, |
| /ĕ/ | pet | /oi/ | noise | | item, |
| /ē/ | bee | /ŏŏ/ | took | | edible, |
| /hw/ | whoop | /ōō/ | boot | | gallop, |
| /ĭ/ | pit | /ou/ | out | | circus |
| /ī/ | pie, by | /th/ | thin | /ər/ | butter |
| /î/ | pier | /th/ | this | | |

*The <u>oo</u> in <u>school</u> sounds like the <u>oo</u> in <u>boot</u>.*

★ Write the sample words from the pronunciation key for these sounds:

1. <u>oi</u> in <u>boil</u> _____

2. <u>o</u> in <u>closed</u> _____

3. <u>o</u> in <u>hot</u> _____

4. <u>a</u> in <u>taking</u> _____

★ Write the word that goes with each sound spelling below. Check your answers in the Spelling Dictionary.

**tooth    July    Tuesday    few**

5. /fyōo/ _____

6. /tōoth/ _____

7. /tōoz′ dē/ _____

8. /jōo lī′/ _____

136

# Ch

Write
Then

1. So
2. Yo
3. "C
4. The
5. A
6. Ne
7. A
8. Too
9. An
10. The
11. A
12. A f
13. You
14. Son

15. Peo
    sou
    The
    and
    follo
    seco
    Can

16. How

# WORDS AT WORK

## Challenge Yourself

**pursue    shrewd    casual    dispute**

Decide which Challenge Word fits each clue. Check your Spelling Dictionary to see if you were right. Then write sentences showing that you understand the meaning of each Challenge Word.

1. T-shirts and jeans are this type of clothing.

2. This often is something your teacher helps you with.

3. A clever person is this.

4. When you chase someone, you do this to them.

## Write to the Point

Pretend you are like Doreen—the new person in school. Help people get to know you. Write a paragraph about yourself. Include details that tell who you are, what you are like, and what you like to do for fun. Use spelling words from this lesson in your paragraph.

**Challenge** Use one or more of the Challenge Words in your paragraph.

## Proofreading

Use the marks to show the errors in the paragraph below. Write the four misspelled words correctly in the blanks.

> On Juli fourth, I ran in a race  It started at noon and was to miles long. I wore my my red, white, and blew shirt  Guess whue won. I did!

| | |
|---|---|
| ⬭ | word is misspelled |
| ⊙ | period is missing |
| ﹥ | take out word |

1. _____

2. _____

3. _____

4. _____

137

# THE BUNTING

Last _____ my class went to Lone Pine State Park for a nature walk. We take these trips to _____ about nature. And they are a fun part of our school _____. Each class trip is a holiday.

At the park a _____ named Jane said she would be our guide. She told us lots of facts about our planet, the _____. She told us what plants and animals to look for. Jane said that we might even see a painted bunting. That is a rare _____ with red, blue, and green feathers.

We _____ only a little way down the trail when showoff Bonnie Williams spotted a fawn. It had white spots on its _____. If only I could find something special, too!

I kept my eyes and ears open. The path turned once, twice, and then a _____ time . I happened to look down at the _____ behind a tall pine tree.

140

At _____, I saw only a wiggly

_____. I watched it _____ and

uncurl. Then I saw one of the most beautiful things

in the _____. I saw a real live painted

bunting. I wanted to yell to the others, but I didn't

say a _____. I didn't want to scare the

painted bunting.

I saw the bird _____ and fly away.
In a flash of color it was gone. No one else saw
the bunting. But I knew that I was one up on
showoff Bonnie Williams.

girl
bird
first
dirt
third
world
work
word
worm
curl
fur
Thursday
turn
learn
earth
were

# Antonyms

An antonym is a word that means the opposite of another word.

*An antonym of <u>small</u> is <u>big</u>.*
*An antonym of <u>thick</u> is <u>thin</u>.*

   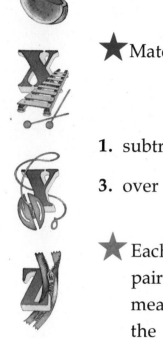      

★Match each word below with its antonym.

**under     add     huge     young**

**1.** subtract _____     **2.** tiny _____

**3.** over _____     **4.** old _____

★Each group of four words below has a pair of antonyms and a pair of synonyms. (Remember that synonyms are words that mean the same.) First write the antonyms together. Then write the synonyms together.

**5. full     forever     empty     always**

antonyms: _____

synonyms: _____

**6. earth     first     world     last**

antonyms: _____

synonyms: _____

**7. study     learn     boy     girl**

antonyms: _____

synonyms: _____

**8. dirty     clean     bird     fowl**

antonyms: _____

synonyms: _____

142

# WORDS AT WORK

## Challenge Yourself

**circular surgeon dessert flourish**

Use your Spelling Dictionary to answer these questions. Then write sentences showing that you understand the meaning of each Challenge Word.

1. Is the trunk of a pine tree circular?

2. Do you think you would see a surgeon in a bird's nest?

3. Do you think you would find grass in a dessert?

4. Do buntings and other birds flourish in wooded areas?

## Write to the Point

You don't have to go into the woods to see nature. Look around you. The sky, the trees, and the animals are all part of nature. Write a paragraph describing one thing you see often in nature. Use spelling words from this lesson in your paragraph.

**Challenge** Use one or more of the Challenge Words in your paragraph.

## Proofreading

Use the marks to show the errors in the paragraph below. Write the four misspelled words correctly in the blanks.

| | |
|---|---|
| ⬭ | word is misspelled |
| ⊙ | period is missing |
| ≡ | letter should be capitalized |

The first bird ate a werm. The second one ate a bug  The therd said bugs made his feathers kurl. he saw a berry in the dert and ate it

1. _____

2. _____

3. _____

4. _____

143

# Lesson 27  Words with /ä/

Listen for /ä/ as you say each word.

father

market

barn

garden

star

sharp

bark

yard

dark

hard

card

start

March

arm

art

heart

1. Which two words begin with the letter a?

_____

2. Which word has the letters th in it?

_____

3. Which word is spelled with a capital letter?

_____

4. Write three words that have two syllables.

_____

_____

5. In which word is /ä/ spelled with the letters ea? _____

6. Which two words begin with the letters st?

_____

7. Which two words have the letters ark in them?

_____

8. Which three words end with the letters ard?

_____

_____

9. Which word begins with the letters sh?

_____

10. Write two words that begin with the letter b.

_____

# Checkpoint

Write a spelling word for each clue.
Then use the Checkpoint Study Plan on page 224.

1. A place where you grow flowers is a ___.

2. Blood is pumped through your ___.

3. A point of light in the night sky is a ___.

4. A place where you buy things is a ___.

5. A short, gruff sound a dog makes is a ___.

6. On a friend's birthday, you send a ___.

7. Something that has an edge that cuts is ___.

8. The month that follows February is ___.

9. It takes three feet to make one ___.

10. A beautiful painting is ___.

11. A place where cows live is a ___.

12. When there is no light, it is ___.

13. Another word for begin is ___.

14. The opposite of easy is ___.

15. She is my mother, he is my ___.

16. Sometimes words that are spelled alike have
    different meanings. They are called homographs.
        This mystery word is two homographs. One
    homograph means a weapon. It comes from
    the Latin word *arma*. The other means a part
    of the body. It comes from the Old German
    word *aram*. Can you guess this word? ___

145

Use each word once to complete this story.

# Annie Oakley

One of the great sharpshooters in Buffalo Bill's Wild West Show was Annie Oakley.

Annie was born on a farm in Ohio on August 13, 1860. Annie's mother and _____ noticed her interest in target shooting. But they never guessed that she would one day be a _____ in Buffalo Bill's show.

Annie grew up like most kids on a farm. She had to feed the animals that lived in the pens and in the _____. She had to pick the _____ vegetables. And she had to go

146

to the _____ to buy the things they needed. But Annie also practiced sharpshooting.

Her father would set up cans in the front _____ for shooting practice. A neighbor watching Annie once said, "She could shoot the _____ off a tree!" The neighbor was right. Annie's good aim and her _____ eyesight made her a local star.

Annie put her whole _____ into her work. She often practiced shooting until it was _____. But all her _____ work helped her become a star.

On _____ 20, 1874, Annie won a shooting contest against champion Frank E. Butler. Later Annie and Frank got married. Then they joined Buffalo Bill's show.

Buffalo Bill used Annie's sharpshooting act to _____ the Wild West Show. One of her most dangerous acts was shooting the thin edge of a playing _____. She did this while holding a rifle in one _____ and hanging from a moving horse with the other!

Annie thought sharpshooting was more than just fancy shooting. She believed it was an _____.

147

*father*
*market*
*barn*
*garden*
*star*
*sharp*
*bark*
*yard*
*dark*
*hard*
*card*
*start*
*March*
*arm*
*art*
*heart*

# Definitions

The meaning of a word is called the <u>definition</u>. Some words have more than one meaning. <u>Heart</u> has two definitions in the Spelling Dictionary.

**Definition 1** ⟶

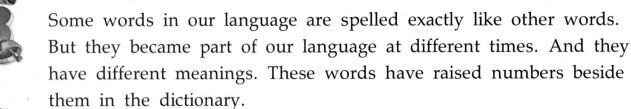

**heart** | härt | —*noun, plural* **hearts**
**1.** The organ in the chest that pumps blood through the body: *The doctor listened to my heart.* **2.** Courage and enthusiasm: *Howard put his whole heart into winning the game.*

⟵ **Definition 2**

★ Read the sample sentences in the two definitions above. The words around the word <u>heart</u> give a clue to its meaning.

Which definition of <u>heart</u> is used in each sentence below?

**1.** Our class lost heart when we lost the game. _____

**2.** My heart beats fast after a race. _____

Some words in our language are spelled exactly like other words. But they became part of our language at different times. And they have different meanings. These words have raised numbers beside them in the dictionary.

**bark¹** | bärk | —*noun, plural* **barks** The sharp, explosive sound made by a dog or fox: *I could hear my dog's bark a mile away.* —*verb* To make the sharp sound a dog makes: *Fido likes to bark at cats.*
**bark²** | bärk | —*noun, plural* **barks** The outer covering of trees and other woody plants: *The bark of a birch tree is thin and peels off easily.*

★ Which definition of <u>bark</u> is used in each sentence below?

**3.** Lassie has a loud bark. _____

**4.** My cat clawed the bark of the tree. _____

148

# WORDS AT WORK

## Challenge Yourself

**carton    starch    artistic    barbecue**

What do you think each underlined Challenge Word means? Check your Spelling Dictionary to see if you are right. Then write sentences showing that you understand the meaning of each Challenge Word.

1. Milk is in a <u>carton</u> or a jug.

2. Too much <u>starch</u> on your shirt will make it stiff.

3. Annie Oakley thought her sharpshooting was <u>artistic</u>.

4. Frank and Annie may have served <u>barbecue</u> at their wedding.

## Write to the Point

Everyone is good at something. Annie Oakley was a good sharpshooter. Are you a good student? A good athlete? Maybe you are a good friend. Write a paragraph telling about what you are good at. Use spelling words from this lesson in your paragraph.

**Challenge** Use one or more of the Challenge Words in your paragraph.

## Proofreading

Use the marks to show the errors in the paragraph below. Write the four misspelled words correctly in the blanks.

| | |
|---|---|
| ⬭ | word is misspelled |
| ⊙ | period is missing |
| ≡ | letter should be capitalized |

In march let's put on a show in our barne. Spot can barck a song, and I'll do carde tricks  Then mary can lead a parade around the gardin.

1. _____

2. _____

3. _____

4. _____

149

# Lesson 28 Words with /oi/

**Listen for /oi/ as you say each word.**

soil

broil

coin

point

boil

choice

noise

voice

spoil

oil

join

boy

toy

joy

enjoy

royal

1. Write the two words in which you hear /s/ but don't see the letter s.

_____ _____

2. Which word ends with the letters al?

_____

3. Write the word in which you hear /z/ but don't see the letter z. _____

4. Write five words that have the letters oil.

_____ _____

_____ _____

_____

5. Which four words end with the last two letters of decoy?

_____ _____

_____ _____

6. Write three words that have the letters oin.

_____ _____

_____

7. Write the two words that begin with a vowel.

_____

# Checkpoint

Write a spelling word for each clue.
Then use the Checkpoint Study Plan on page 224.

1. To cook directly under or over heat is to ___.

2. Seeds are planted in ___.

3. Loud sounds make lots of ___.

4. Something you like is something you ___.

5. "Fit for a king or queen" means ___.

6. A liquid you need to run a car is ___.

7. To take part in something with others is to ___.

8. A penny, a dime, or a quarter is a ___.

9. The tip is the ___.

10. If you get to choose, you have a ___.

11. A male child is a ___.

12. To ruin is to ___.

13. Something you play with is a ___.

14. Another word for happiness is ___.

15. You talk and sing with your ___.

16. This mystery word tells what happens when liquid gets very hot. It comes from the Latin word *bulla. Bulla* meant bubble. When a liquid gets very hot, we can see large bubbles in it. The bubbles move about very quickly. When liquid gets hot and begins to bubble, it begins to ___.

Use each word once to complete this story.

# A Camping Tale

Soon after May had caught the fish, she realized she was alone. She yelled until she almost lost her _____ . But no one answered. She was lost. And there was no one to _____ the way. Her camping trip had become a nightmare.

"I might not _____ it," she thought, "but I guess I'll have to make it alone. I don't have any other _____!"

At first, May jumped at every _____ in the woods. But soon she got used to the noises.

May was very hungry. That made her think about the _____ purse in her pocket. But the coins might have been _____ money. They wouldn't buy any food in the woods. At least she had a sleeping bag and a few supplies. She would be all right.

"The first thing I'll do," she thought, "is build a fire. Then I'll _____ water for cocoa. I don't have any _____ to fry the fish. I'll have to _____ the fish I caught. I'll cook a _____ feast!"

152

May had just finished broiling the fish when it began to rain. She didn't want the rain to _____ her breakfast. She pushed a branch into the soft _____. Then she put her sleeping bag over it to make a tent. It was warm inside. May began to yawn. Soon she was fast asleep.

When she woke up, a _____ was looking into the tent. "Breakfast is ready," said her brother. "Aren't you going to _____ us?"

May was in her family's tent. It was a bright morning. The birds were singing for _____. She laughed. It was only a dream after all.

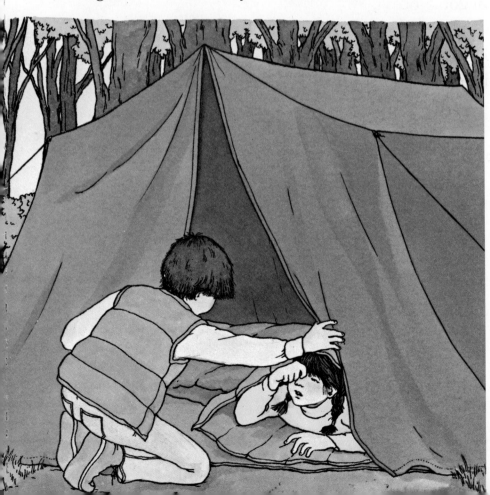

soil
broil
coin
point
boil
choice
noise
voice
spoil
oil
join
boy
toy
joy
enjoy
royal

# Review of Capitals

Use a capital letter to begin:

- *the first word of a sentence*  ● *the word I*
- *the names of people and pets*  ● *the names of cities and states*
- *the names of streets*

⭐ Unscramble the spelling words as you write each sentence below. Put capital letters where they belong.

1. martha felt yloar on her birthday.

_____

2. i noyej visiting minneapolis.

_____

3. fido makes a lot of sonie!

_____

4. vincent has a good ocevi.

_____

5. can you tonip out mallory street?

_____

6. shall we robil this chicken?

_____

7. this nico was made in colorado.

_____

8. mrs. hays bought a yto for her baby oby.

_____

9. kevin and i want to nioj the team.

_____

154

## Challenge Yourself

| | |
|---|---|
| moisten | poisonous |
| rejoice | enjoyment |

Use your Spelling Dictionary to answer these questions. Then write sentences showing that you understand the meaning of each Challenge Word.

1. Would you <u>moisten</u> a stamp?

2. Are <u>poisonous</u> snakes dangerous?

3. Did May <u>rejoice</u> when she realized she was lost?

4. Does a nightmare usually bring <u>enjoyment</u>?

## Write to the Point

Think about the things people do on camping trips. Then write a paragraph telling what May did after she woke up. You might begin by telling what she had for breakfast. Use spelling words from this lesson in your paragraph.

**Challenge** Use one or more of the Challenge Words in your paragraph.

## Proofreading

Use the marks to show the errors in the paragraph below. Write the four misspelled words correctly in the blanks.

| | |
|---|---|
| ◯ | word is misspelled |
| ⊙ | period is missing |
| ＝ | letter should be capitalized |

I dreamed I lived in a royle castle. I had every toy a boi could want. nothing could spoyal my joy Then the voyse of my brother james woke me up

1. _____

2. _____

3. _____

4. _____

155

# Lesson 29 Contractions

Say each word.

hasn't
aren't
couldn't
didn't
doesn't
hadn't
haven't
mustn't
shouldn't
wasn't
weren't
isn't
wouldn't

won't
don't

can't

1. Which two words begin with /k/?

2. Write the three words that have the letters <u>ould</u>.

3. Write the two words that begin with a vowel.

4. Write the two words that have the <u>o</u> spelling of /ō/.

5. Which word begins with the letter <u>m</u>?

6. Which three words begin with the letter <u>h</u>?

7. Which three words begin with the letter <u>d</u>?

8. Which four words begin with the letter <u>w</u>?

# Checkpoint

Write a spelling word for each clue.
Then use the Checkpoint Study Plan on page 224.

1. are     + not = ___

2. did     + not = ___

3. had     + not = ___

4. has     + not = ___

5. was     + not = ___

6. is       + not = ___

7. does    + not = ___

8. have    + not = ___

9. must    + not = ___

10. were    + not = ___

11. will     + not = ___

12. do      + not = ___

13. would  + not = ___

14. cannot        = ___

15. The first mystery word is a form of the verb <u>can</u>. It used to be spelled <u>coud</u>. This word plus the contraction of <u>not</u> is ___.

16. The second mystery word is a form of the verb <u>shall</u>. It used to be spelled <u>sholde</u>. The word plus the contraction of <u>not</u> is ___.

Use each word once to complete this story.

# THE CHALLENGE

Billy watched Dave, waiting to see what he would do next. This was the first time he had faced Dave. Billy _____ happy about it. "If only I _____ said yes to his challenge," he thought. "Then I _____ be in this mess."

"You _____ going to back down?" Dave asked. Billy knew that he could not back down now. He just _____ back down. A lot of his friends were watching him. They _____ going to leave until it was all over. They had tried to tell him about Dave. "You _____ heard?" they had asked. "He's tough. He _____ like losing."

Billy _____ like to lose either. His hands were sweaty. His knees were shaking. "I _____ help it," he thought. "I want to beat this guy." Billy rubbed his hands on his clothes. "Be steady," he told himself. "If there is one thing I must not do, I _____ look scared.

158

I _____ want to make it easy for Dave to win. Besides, it _____ be the end of the world if I lose."

Then Dave made his move. Billy knew that it was the wrong one. "He _____ got a chance now," he thought.

Billy grinned. "You _____ have done that, Dave," he said. "I'm going to beat you. But don't worry. It _____ going to hurt for long."

In one move, Billy cleared the checkerboard of Dave's pieces. The game was over. Billy had met the challenge.

hasn't
aren't
couldn't
didn't
doesn't
hadn't
haven't
mustn't
shouldn't
wasn't
weren't
isn't
wouldn't
won't
don't
can't

# Apostrophes

A contraction is a shortened form of two words. An apostrophe (')
in a contraction shows that a letter or letters have been left out.

| Two Words | Contraction | Left Out |
|-----------|-------------|----------|
| are not | aren't | o |
| is not | isn't | o |

★ Write the contractions of the words in the list below.

1. could not _____

2. have not _____

3. do not _____

4. had not _____

★ Write two sentences using the contractions <u>wouldn't</u> and <u>won't</u>.

5. wouldn't _____

6. won't _____

7. What are the two words for <u>wouldn't</u>? _____

8. What are the two words for <u>won't</u>? _____

★ Write the correct contraction in each sentence.

9. Sasha (wasn't/weren't) home yesterday.

_____

10. My other friends (wasn't/weren't) home either!

_____

★ Sometimes a contraction is made from one word.

11. What is the one word from which <u>can't</u> is

made? _____

**160**

## Challenge Yourself

**there'll    how'd    we'd    there'd**

Use your Spelling Dictionary to answer these questions. Then write sentences showing that you understand the meaning of each Challenge Word.

1. Is there'll a contraction for the words there will?

2. Is how'd a contraction for the words how did?

3. Is we'd a contraction for we did?

4. Is there'd a contraction for the words there did?

## Write to the Point

Rules tell how you play a game and what you can and cannot do. Write three rules for a game you know. An example of a soccer rule is "Don't touch the ball with your hands." Use spelling words from this lesson in your rules.

**Challenge** Use one or more of the Challenge Words in your rules.

## Proofreading

Use the marks to show the errors in the paragraph below. Write the four misspelled words correctly in the blanks.

| | |
|---|---|
| ◯ | word is misspelled |
| ⊙ | period is missing |
| ＝ | letter should be capitalized |

This checkerboard has'nt been used in ten years  Is'nt it in great shape? it doesn't look old. My Aunt Rosa won'nt let anyone use it but me. I musn't ruin it

1. _____

2. _____

3. _____

4. _____

# Lesson 30 Words in Review

**A.** tooth
true
move
knew
July
few
used

**B.** dirt
worm
curl
learn
were

**C.** sharp
heart

**D.** voice
enjoy

★ Use a piece of paper for the starred activities.

**1.** In Lesson 25 you studied five ways to spell /o͞o/: **oo, ue, o, ew, u.** And you studied two ways to spell /yo͞o/: **ew, u_e.** Write the words in list A.

_____    _____

_____    _____

_____

**2.** In Lesson 26 you studied five ways to spell /û/: **i, o, u, ea, e.** Write the words in list B.

_____    _____

_____    _____

_____

★**3.** Now write the words in lists A and B. Look them up in the Spelling Dictionary and write the sound spelling next to each word.

**4.** In Lesson 27 you studied two ways to spell /ä/ **a, ea.** Write the words in list C.

_____    _____

**5.** In Lesson 28 you studied two ways to spell /oi/: **oi, oy.** Write the words in list D.

_____    _____

★**6.** Now write a sentence for each review word in lists C and D.

★**7.** Write sentences for the words in lists A and B.

★**8.** Write all the review words in alphabetical order.

162

# Writer's Workshop

## A How-To Paragraph

A how-to paragraph gives information about how to do something. In a how-to paragraph, writers give step-by-step instructions, using words such as <u>first</u>, <u>second</u>, <u>next</u>, <u>then</u>, and <u>finally</u>. Here is Una's paragraph. In it she tells how to make her favorite sandwich.

> ### How to Make My Favorite Sandwich
> I have a recipe for a great sandwich. I call it my Super Sandwich. To make my Super Sandwich, the first thing you do is get some bread, peanut butter, honey, and bananas. Second, cut the bananas into very thin slices. Next, spread the peanut butter on one side of each piece of bread. Finally, pour a little honey on the peanut butter, add the bananas, and put the two slices of bread together. Now you can take a big bite!

To write her how-to paragraph, Una followed the steps in the writing process. She began with a **Prewriting** activity. She used a flow chart to list the steps for making her favorite sandwich. This helped her know the order in which to write the steps. Part of Una's flow chart is shown here. Study what Una did.

| 1 | Get bread, peanut butter, honey, bananas. |
|---|---|
| 2 | Cut the bananas. |
| 3 | Spread the peanut butter on the bread. |

**It's Your Turn**

Get ready to write your own how-to paragraph. Think of something you know how to do. After you have decided what to write about, make a flow chart. Then follow the other steps in the writing process—**Writing**, **Revising**, **Proofreading**, and **Publishing**.

# Lesson 31 Words with /ô/

**Listen for /ô/ as you say each word.**

autumn

August


born

fork

morning

sport

popcorn

storm

north

corner

before


door

floor


pour

four


quart

1. Which word begins with /kw/?

_____

2. Write two words that begin with a vowel.

_____

3. Which two words end with the last three letters of <u>tour</u>?

_____

4. Write three words that begin with the letter <u>f</u>.

_____

5. Write four words that have the letters <u>orn</u>.

_____

_____

6. Which word ends with the letters <u>th</u>?

_____

7. Which word begins with a consonant and ends with a vowel? _____

8. Write two words that begin with the letter <u>s</u>.

_____

9. Which two words end with the letters <u>oor</u>?

_____

10. Which word always begins with a capital letter?

# Checkpoint

Write a spelling word for each clue.
Then use the Checkpoint Study Plan on page 224.

1. You eat breakfast in the ___.

2. The kind of corn you eat at the movies is ___.

3. The place where two streets meet is the ___.

4. Your birthday is the day you were ___.

5. Another name for the season fall is ___.

6. Outside is the ground, inside is the ___.

7. Strong winds and rain are a ___.

8. To get into a room, you open the ___.

9. The opposite of south is ___.

10. The number after three is ___.

11. To put milk into a glass is to ___.

12. Another word for game is ___.

13. Two pints make one ___.

14. You eat with a knife, spoon, and ___.

15. The opposite of after is ___.

16. Perhaps the greatest Roman emperor was Caesar Augustus. *Augustus* meant "very great man." Caesar Augustus made sure that he would always be remembered. He had the Romans name a certain month after him. This month still has his name. Guess it, and you will know the mystery word. ___

165

# Alphabetical Order

Put words that begin with the same letter into alphabetical order by using the second letter.

h<u>a</u>mmer     h<u>o</u>rse

The letter <u>a</u> comes before <u>o</u>, so <u>hammer</u> comes before <u>horse</u>.

Sometimes the first and second letters of a word are the same. When this happens, use the third letter to put words in alphabetical order.

tr<u>a</u>in     tr<u>i</u>m

The letter <u>a</u> comes before <u>i</u>, so <u>train</u> comes before <u>trim</u>.

★ Look at the third letter of each word in the lists below. Then write the words in alphabetical order.

**1. autumn    aunt    August**

**2. fork    four    foggy**

_____

_____

_____

★ Put the words below each sentence in alphabetical order. Then write the sentence using those words.

**3.** Ray ____ weeks learning the ____ of jogging last ____ .

(sport, spent, spring) _____

_____

**4.** ____ ____ ran two minutes ____ she ____ to fall ____ .

(began, Beatrice, before, behind, Becker) _____

_____

## Challenge Yourself

**ornament  wharf  coarse  corridor**

Decide which Challenge Word fits each clue. Check your Spelling Dictionary to see if you were right. Then write sentences showing that you understand the meaning of each Challenge Word.

1. You could expect to see water and boats at one of these.

2. You walk through one to get to another part of a building.

3. This is a kind of decoration.

4. This word describes things that are not smooth.

## Write to the Point

It would be fun to live in the Land of Flipflop. Or would it? Write a paragraph telling why you would or would not want to live in Flipflop. Give at least two reasons that explain how you made your decision. Use spelling words from this lesson in your paragraph.

**Challenge** Use one or more of the Challenge Words in your paragraph.

## Proofreading

Use the marks to show the errors in the paragraph below. Write the four misspelled words correctly in the blanks.

One Awgust morning in Flipflop, I saw a dog using a foork   He was on the flore eating a book about New mexico. that was befor I woke up.

| | word is misspelled |
| :-: | :-- |
| ⊙ | period is missing |
| ≡ | letter should be capitalized |

1. _____

2. _____

3. _____

4. _____

169

# THE FROG PRINCE

Use each word once to complete this story.

Marci's brother Ben liked to _____ pictures. One day he drew a picture of a green _____. It had a little crown on its head. Ben _____ the picture to Marci.

Ben was deaf. So Ben and Marci used their hands to talk to each other. "If you kiss a frog, it will turn into a prince," Ben signed to Marci with his hands. She was sure he was grinning at her.

"That's just silly _____," Marci signed back. But soon she began to think about a frog turning into a handsome prince. He was six feet _____. His _____ hands held the reins of a horse. A _____ sword hung at his side.

"Aren't you ready yet?" her mother called. Marci's dream ended.

Every Saturday, Marci's mother went shopping at the _____. Marci _____ went. Ben usually came _____, too. Today, Mother and Ben _____ food. Marci wanted to be by herself. She went for a _____.

172

It was warm. So Marci took _____ her coat. But she was still hot.

She walked to the pond in the center of the mall. "Maybe it's cooler by the _____," she thought. Marci sat down on the wall. Suddenly a frog jumped from the pond to the wall beside her.

"Could it be a prince?" Marci wondered. "Should I really kiss it?"

As she reached for the frog, a voice yelled, "That frog doesn't _____ to you! Put it down!"

A police officer rushed over. "What are you doing to that frog?" she asked.

"Nothing," Marci said. "I wanted to help him, _____ he might be . . ." She stopped. It sounded so silly. She got up and sadly walked away.

"Now I'll never be sure," Marci thought.

frog
long
along
off
belong
strong
water
always
mall
tall
talk
walk
bought
brought
draw
because

# Subeljcts and Predicates

The subject of a sentence tells who or what is doing the action or is being talked about.

(Sally) danced.

(The cat) jumped off the chair.

The predicate of a sentence tells what the subject does or did.

Sally _danced_.

The cat _jumped off the chair_.

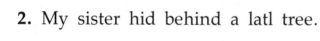 Unscramble the spelling words as you write each sentence below. Then circle the subject and underline the predicate.

**1.** Jack dived into the ratwe.

_____

**2.** My sister hid behind a latl tree.

_____

**3.** Harry tughob a baseball.

_____

**4.** Marcia owns that toy gofr.

_____

**5.** Mrs. Martin took a nogl vacation.

_____

**6.** A orntgs wind blew across the lake.

_____

**7.** I will wrad a picture of you.

_____

**8.** The old clock fell fof the shelf.

_____

## Challenge Yourself

**sausage    broth    dawdle    install**

Use your Spelling Dictionary to answer these questions. Then write sentences showing that you understand the meaning of each Challenge Word.

1. Would you comb your hair with a <u>sausage</u>?

2. Would you find <u>broth</u> in vegetable soup?

3. If you were in a hurry, would you <u>dawdle</u>?

4. Should you <u>install</u> a stove before you turn it on?

## Write to the Point

Do you think a prince would have appeared if Marci had kissed the frog? Write a new ending for the story. Start your paragraph with these words—"Marci reached for the frog and _____." Use spelling words from this lesson in your ending.

**Challenge** Use one or more of the Challenge Words in your ending.

## Proofreading

Use the marks to show the errors in the paragraph below. Write the four misspelled words correctly in the blanks.

| | |
|---|---|
| ◯ | word is misspelled |
| ≡ | letter should be capitalized |
| ϑ | take out word |

   Mom and i allways walk to the mall. We tawk as we stroll along the path by by the watter. it's nice becuz we're together.

1. _____

2. _____

3. _____

4. _____

# Lesson 33 Words with /ou/

**Listen for /ou/ as you say each word.**

hour

sound

ground

about

house

around

count

our

found


owl

down

power

brown

tower

town

flower

1. Write two words that sound exactly the same but are not spelled the same.

_____  _____

2. Write three words that end with the last three letters of <u>clown</u>. _____

_____

3. Which word ends with /s/? _____

4. Write two words that end with the letter <u>t</u>.

_____  _____

5. Write two words that begin with the vowel <u>o</u>.

_____  _____

6. Which three words end with the letters <u>er</u>?

_____  _____

_____

7. Write four words that have the last four letters of <u>round</u>.

_____  _____

_____  _____

8. Write the two words in which you see the letter <u>a</u> but don't hear /ă/ or /ā/.

_____

# Checkpoint

Write a spelling word for each clue.
Then use the Checkpoint Study Plan on page 224.

1. You tell time with a second, a minute, and an ____.

2. Another word for almost and nearly is ____.

3. Another word for land and earth is ____.

4. A very tall part of a building is a ____.

5. A bird that says "Whooo?" is an ____.

6. If you're going in a circle, you're going ____.

7. Your home is your ____.

8. Part of a plant with petals is a ____.

9. Something you hear is a ____.

10. The opposite of up is ____.

11. The opposite of lost is ____.

12. The color of chocolate is ____.

13. Will you come to ____ party?

14. Another word for strength is ____.

15. To say numbers in order is to ____.

16. Long ago, people built fences and walls around cities. These fences and walls protected the people from enemies and thieves. In the Old English language, a fence or wall was called a *toun*. Soon, a fence or wall became a sign that people lived nearby. So a place where people lived became known as a *toun*. That is what the mystery word means today. Can you guess it? ____

Use each word once to complete this story.

# THE OWL

Of all the birds, owls are _____ the easiest to recognize. They all have large, round heads. They have big eyes that look straight ahead.

Owls come in several colors. Snowy owls are white. Owls of the deep rain forest are often dark _____ in color.

At last _____ , there were 132 different kinds of owls. Scientists think some owls are in danger of becoming extinct. They feel it is

_____ duty to protect the owl. Owls are not only beautiful. They are also useful to people. Owls help farmers. They eat rodents that hurt the crops.

Owls can be _____ almost every place in the world. An _____ will make its home in a tree or in a barn. Some owls will even nest on top of a water _____ near a busy _____ .

Most owls hunt for food at night. The owls' eyes are very large, so they see well in the dark. Owls also have very good hearing. With their sharp hearing and keen sight, they fly above the _____ looking for small animals, such as mice and rats. Owls are meat eaters. They will never eat a plant or a _____ .
An owl can swoop _____ without making a _____ . Once caught, an animal has little chance of getting away from the _____ of the owl's grip. In one _____ an owl can catch two or three mice.

Owls are as good at catching mice as cats are. But owls do not make good _____ pets. Owls need room to fly _____ .

179

hour
sound
ground
about
house
around
count
our
found
owl
down
power
brown
tower
town
flower

# Review of Capitals

Use a capital letter to begin:

- *the first word of a sentence*   • *the word I*
- *the names of people and pets*   • *the names of cities and states*
- *the names of streets*

★ Write each sentence. Put capital letters where they belong.

1. todd lives in lexington.

2. his friend, graham, lives around the corner.

3. every saturday, they get together.

4. graham and todd spend hours exploring.

5. they always take brown bags full of snacks.

6. saturday, at tower avenue, they heard a sound.

7. graham's dog, rovereena, had found them.

8. "you can always count on rovereena to try to get into the act!"

said graham.

# WORDS AT WORK

## Challenge Yourself

**doubtful devour bough wildflower**

What do you think each underlined Challenge Word means? Check your Spelling Dictionary to see if you are right. Then write sentences showing that you understand the meaning of each Challenge Word.

1. It is <u>doubtful</u> that an owl would be a good house pet.

2. A hungry owl will <u>devour</u> a big meal.

3. A little owl sat on the <u>bough</u> of a tree.

4. An owl would rather eat a mouse than a <u>wildflower</u>.

## Write to the Point

An owl would not make a very good pet. Owls need space to fly and look for food. There are many animals that do make good pets, however. Write a paragraph telling which animal you think makes the best pet. Use spelling words from this lesson in your paragraph.

**Challenge** Use one or more of the Challenge Words in your paragraph.

## Proofreading

Use the marks to show the errors in the paragraph below. Write the four misspelled words correctly in the blanks.

> ⬭ word is misspelled
> ⊙ period is missing
> ≡ letter should be capitalized

We heard a strange sownd. we looked around the howse   We found an owle stuck in our chimney. It took an hour to free the big broun bird

1. _____

2. _____

3. _____

4. _____

181

# Lesson 34 /î/, /â/, and /ī/

Listen for /î/ or /â/ or /ī/ as you say each word.

hear

dear

ear

near

year

here

deer

★

stairs

air

chair

hair

care

where

★

tire

fire

wire

1. Write two words that begin with the letter <u>d</u> and sound exactly alike but are spelled differently.

_____

2. Write two words that begin with the letter <u>h</u> and sound exactly alike but are spelled differently.

_____

3. Write three words that end with the last three letters of <u>hire</u>. _____

_____

4. Write the word that begins with /hw/.

_____

5. Which four words have the letters <u>air</u>?

_____

_____

6. Write the word that starts with /k/.

_____

7. Write five words that have the letters <u>ear</u>.

_____

_____

_____

8. Write the word that sounds exactly like <u>hare</u>.

182

# Checkpoint

Write a spelling word for each clue.
Then use the Checkpoint Study Plan on page 224.

1. You hear with an ____.

2. It takes 365 days to make one ____.

3. You drink water, and you breathe ____.

4. To go up to the next floor, you climb the ____.

5. An animal that lives in the forest is a ____.

6. When something burns it is on ____.

7. Don't trip over the telephone ____.

8. Something that grows on your head is ____.

9. Begin a letter with the word ____.

10. If you worry about someone, you ____.

11. When you listen, you ____.

12. The opposite of far is ____.

13. The opposite of there is ____.

14. You ask when, what, why, and ____.

15. Dad changed the flat ____.

16. Have you ever played the telephone game?
    One person whispers something to another
    person who whispers it to another, and
    so on. Often, the last person hears a very
    different message. This mystery word started
    as the Greek word *cathedra*. *Cathedra* meant
    seat. The French changed it to *chaiere*. The
    English changed it, too. Can you guess it? ____

**183**

Use each word once to complete this poem.

# A Strange Story

Come sit _____ me, _____ children.

Come sit right over _____ .

I have a little story,

I tell just once a _____ .

Put a big log on the _____ .

Come close to my little _____ .

And you will hear a story

That's going to curl your _____ .

Take _____ to listen closely.

Let me have your _____ .

This is the strangest story

That you may ever _____ !

I was on my way to go to bed.

I was halfway up the stairs,

When a herd of _____ came running down

With fourteen polar bears!

Before I could catch a breath of _____ ,

Before I could go one step higher,

What do you think went rolling past?

A big, round, tow truck _____ .

(A monkey tried to lasso it

With a lasso made of _____ !)

How did those animals get there?

_____ did those animals go?

I've asked myself a hundred times,

But still I do not know!

Some nights when it's time to go to bed,

And I start to climb the _____ ,

I think I hear the echo

Of deer and polar bears!

185

hear
dear
ear
near
year
here
deer
stairs
air
chair
hair
care
where
tire
fire
wire

# Dictionary Review

The pronunciation key of a dictionary uses letters and symbols to show how words are pronounced. Look at the pronunciation key on page 196 of the Spelling Dictionary.

★ Below are three sounds from the pronunciation key. Match each of these words with a sound from the pronunciation key.

stairs　fire　high　year　where　tire　here　hair　near

1. â as in <u>care</u> _____

2. ī as in <u>pie</u> _____

3. î as in <u>pier</u> _____

★ Look at the third letter of each word. Then write the words in each group in alphabetical order.

4. deer　deck　dear

5. hear　here　held

★ Write these words in alphabetical order. Use first, second, and third letters.

6. you　where　year　which

7. care　wire　air　chair

186

# WORDS AT WORK

## Challenge Yourself

**careless    dreary    dairy    inspire**

Decide which Challenge Word fits each clue. Check your Spelling Dictionary to see if you were right. Then write sentences showing that you understand the meaning of each Challenge Word.

1. A beautiful sunset can often do this to an artist.

2. Cows are at one of these.

3. If you do not pay attention to what you do, you are this.

4. If a day is dark and cloudy, you can use this word to describe it.

## Write to the Point

Write a poem that tells a story. It can rhyme, but it doesn't have to. Your story can be strange or simple. You may want to use one of the lines from "A Strange Story" to start your poem. Use spelling words from this lesson in your poem.

**Challenge** Use one or more of the Challenge Words in your poem.

## Proofreading

Use the marks to show the errors in the paragraph below. Write the four misspelled words correctly in the blanks.

| ◯ | word is misspelled |
|---|---|
| ≡ | letter should be capitalized |
| ✓ | take out word |

On winter nights i like to sit in my chair neer the fier. The aire outside may be cold, but I don't care. in hear it's warm and and cozy.

1. _____

2. _____

3. _____

4. _____

# Lesson 35 Adding er and est

**Say each word.**

stronger

strongest

taller

tallest

greater

greatest

longer

longest

sharper

sharpest


funnier

funniest

dirtier

dirtiest

hotter

hottest

**Complete the word equations.**

1. tall     +   er   = _____

2. long    +   er   = _____

3. great   +   er   = _____

4. sharp   +   er   = _____

5. strong   +   er   = _____


6. tall     +   est   = _____

7. long    +   est   = _____

8. great   +   est   = _____

9. sharp   +   est   = _____

10. strong   +   est   = _____


11. dirty   − y + i   +   er   = _____

12. funny   − y + i   +   er   = _____


13. dirty   − y + i   +   est   = _____

14. funny   − y + i   +   est   = _____


15. hot     + t + er   = _____


16. hot     + t + est   = _____

# Checkpoint

Write a spelling word for each clue.
Then use the Checkpoint Study Plan on page 224.

1. If I am shorter than you, you are ___.

2. If John is taller than both of us, he is the ___.

3. The pencil with the pointiest point is the ___.

4. The silliest joke is the ___.

5. The one that has more strength is ___.

6. Pull the taffy to make it ___ .

7. The one that is the most wonderful is the ___.

8. The opposite of weakest is ___.

9. The opposite of sadder is ___.

10. The opposite of colder is ___.

11. The opposite of coldest is ___.

12. You say long, longer, ___.

13. You say great, ___ , greatest.

14. The opposite of duller is ___.

15. This mystery word means "not clean." It used to be spelled *dritti*. But people began to change its spelling. They made the first <u>i</u> change places with the <u>r</u>. Then they changed the final <u>i</u> to <u>y</u>. However, when <u>er</u> or <u>est</u> are added to the word, the <u>y</u> turns back to <u>i</u>. If you add <u>er</u> to the mystery word, you get ___.

16. Add <u>est</u> to the mystery word and get ___.

189

# Big Splash

Use each word once to complete this story.

Ali, Sue, and Ted were playing in the park. Ali said, "Wow, it's hot for spring !"

Ted wiped his face and said, "It's

_____ than it's been all month."

"It's the _____ it's ever been," cried Sue. She gave a sharp whistle. Ali gave an even _____ one. But both girls had to cover their ears. Ted's whistle was the

_____ of all.

"Oh, Ted. You think you're so great," said Sue.

"You think you're _____ than anyone," cried Ali.

"Well, my whistle was the _____," boasted Ted. "But I'll show you. Let's have a real contest. Let's play tug of war."

Each one wanted to win. Sue was strong.

But Ted thought he was _____

than Sue. And Ali thought she was the

_____.

You don't have to be tall to be strong. Ali wasn't very tall. Sue was _____ than she was. And Ted was the _____.

"Let's put this mud puddle between us," said Ted. "The loser will fall and get dirty."

"I bet you'll get _____ than I will," said Sue.

"You'll be the _____ of all," cried Ali.

Ted and Sue were first. They pulled the rope for a long time. Sue and Ali were next. They pulled for an even _____ time. Ted and Ali were last. Their contest was the _____.

Finally, Ali pulled Ted into the mud. He fell with a big splash. The mud flew. There were big spots on Ali's face. Sue had mud on her sweater.

"You may be the winner, Ali, but you sure look funny," said Sue.

"No _____ than you," said Ali.

Ted just sat in the puddle. "I must look the _____ of all!" he laughed.

191

stronger
strongest
taller
tallest
greater
greatest
longer
longest
sharper
sharpest
funnier
funniest
dirtier
dirtiest
hotter
hottest

# Adjectives

An adjective describes a noun or pronoun by telling what kind, how many, or which one.

*The <u>strong</u> man lifted the box.*
*Mike is <u>strong</u>.*

Add <u>er</u> to many adjectives to compare two people or things.

*Cliff is <u>stronger</u> than Mike.*

Add <u>est</u> to many adjectives to compare more than two people or things.

*Paul is the <u>strongest</u> of all.*

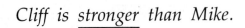 Write the sentences below. Use these words to fill in the blanks.

**greater    hotter    funniest    tallest**

**1.** Sharon tells the ____ jokes we've heard.

_____

_____

**2.** The sun is ____ today than it was yesterday.

_____

_____

**3.** Gilly is the ____ girl on the basketball team.

_____

_____

**4.** Twenty is ____ than ten.

# WORDS AT WORK

## Challenge Yourself

**weirder   weirdest   shakier   shakiest**

What do you think each underlined Challenge Word means? Check your Spelling Dictionary to see if you are right. Then write sentences showing that you understand the meaning of each Challenge Word.

1. Which is <u>weirder</u>—blue hair or a green face?

2. The shadows made the <u>weirdest</u> shapes on the wall.

3. The chair with the short leg is <u>shakier</u> than the other.

4. My chair is the <u>shakiest</u> of all.

## Write to the Point

In "Big Splash" Ali, Sue, and Ted had a contest. Think of a contest you would like to have. Make a sign announcing the contest. Tell where and when it will be held and what the prize will be. Use spelling words from this lesson in your sign.

**Challenge** Use one or more of the Challenge Words in your sign.

## Proofreading

Use the marks to show the errors in the paragraph below. Write the four misspelled words correctly in the blanks.

spring is the greatist season. The

sun shines stronger and hoter  The

days are longger. The trees and

grass grow taler and faster  mr. Ho

told us why this happens.

| | |
|---|---|
| ◯ | word is misspelled |
| ⊙ | period is missing |
| = | letter should be capitalized |

1. _____

2. _____

3. _____

4. _____

193

# Lesson 36 Words in Review

**A.** corner

floor

pour

quart

**B.** strong

bought

because

talk

**C.** count

tower

**D.** near

here

deer

stairs

where

wire

★ Use a piece of paper for the starred activities.

**1.** In Lesson 31 you studied five ways to spell /ô/: **au, o, oo, ou, a.** Write the words in list A, which show four of these spellings.

_____  _____

_____

**2.** In Lesson 32 you studied five ways to spell /ô/: **o, a, ou, aw, au.** Write the words in list B, which show four of these spellings.

_____  _____

_____

★ **3.** Write a sentence for each word in lists A and B.

**4.** In Lesson 33 you studied two ways to spell /ou/: **ou, ow.** Write the words in list C.

_____

**5.** In Lesson 34 you studied three ways to spell /î/: **ea, e, ee.** You studied three ways to spell /â/: **ai, a, e.** And you studied one way to spell /ī/: **i_e.** Write the words in list D, which show some of these spellings.

_____  _____

_____  _____

★ **6.** Now write the review words in lists C and D. Look up each word in the Spelling Dictionary and write the sound spelling next to each word.

194

# Writer's Workshop

## A Narrative

A narrative that continues another story is called a sequel. A sequel is a whole story with a beginning, a middle, and an end. It usually has the same characters and setting as the original story. Here is Julio's sequel to the story "The Frog Prince" on pages 172 and 173.

### Marci Returns

Marci could not forget about the frog. So the next time she was in the mall, she walked by the pond. She looked for the frog, but it was not there. When she saw the police officer, she asked, "Where has the frog gone?" The officer scratched his head and said, "That's a real mystery. That frog disappeared two days ago, the same day we found a sword in the pond."

To write his narrative, Julio followed the steps in the writing process. He began with a **Prewriting** activity using a story map. The story map helped him decide what would happen at the beginning, the middle, and the end of his sequel. Julio's story map is shown here. Study what Julio did.

**Beginning**
Marci returns to the mall.

**Middle**
She can't find the frog.

**End**
She learns what happened from the police officer.

**It's Your Turn**

Get ready to write your own sequel to a story. It can be any story that you have read or heard before. After you have decided on a story to continue, make a story map. Then follow the other steps in the writing process—**Writing, Revising, Proofreading,** and **Publishing.**

# SPELLING
# Dic·tion·ar·y

| | Pronunciation Key | | | | |
|---|---|---|---|---|---|
| /ă/ | pat | /ŏ/ | pot | /ŭ/ | cut |
| /ā/ | pay | /ō/ | toe | /û/ | urge |
| /â/ | care | /ô/ | paw, | /zh/ | vision |
| /ä/ | father | | for | /ə/ | about, |
| /ĕ/ | pet | /oi/ | noise | | item, |
| /ē/ | bee | /ŏŏ/ | took | | edible, |
| /hw/ | whoop | /ōō/ | boot | | gallop, |
| /ĭ/ | pit | /ou/ | out | | circus |
| /ī/ | pie, by | /th/ | thin | /ər/ | butter |
| /î/ | pier | /th/ | this | | |

able | ago

## A

**a•ble** | ā′ bəl | —*adjective* **abler, ablest**
Having enough skill to do
something; capable: *Arnold, the
circus elephant, is able to stand on
his head.*

**a•bout** | ə **bout**′ | —*preposition* Of;
concerning: *Do you know the story
about Goldilocks and the three
bears?*—*adverb* Almost; nearly: *This
recipe makes about 16 brownies.*

**add** | ăd | —*verb* **added, adding** To find
the sum of: *When you add 2 and 6,
the sum is 8.*

**ad•dress** | ə **drĕs**′ | or | **ăd**′ res′ | —*noun,
plural* **addresses** The place where
a person lives or receives mail: *I
want to mail a birthday card to Tom,
but I don't know his address.*

**ad•mire** | ăd **mīr**′ | —*verb* **admired,
admiring** **1.** To respect: *I admire
your courage.* **2.** To look at or
regard with pleasure and

appreciation: *Our class admired the
drawings of the animals.*

**a•do•be** | ə **dō**′ bē | —*noun, plural* **adobes**
**1.** Brick made of straw and clay that
is dried in the sun. **2.** A building
made out of these bricks: *The girl
lived in a house made of adobe.*

**a•fraid** | ə **frād**′ | —*adjective* Frightened;
full of fear: *I'm not afraid of the
dark.*

**af•ter** | **ăf**′ tər | or | **äf**′ tər | —*preposition*
Following; at a later time than: *Mom
said I could go to Pete's after dinner.*

**a•gain** | ə **gĕn**′ | —*adverb* Once more;
another time: *It's time for a spelling
test again.*

**a•gent** | **ā**′ jənt | —*noun, plural* **agents**
**1.** A person who acts for another
person, company, or government: *His
father is an insurance agent.*
**2.** Something that produces or
causes a certain effect: *Too much
rain is the agent of a flood.*

**a•go** | ə **gō**′ | —*adjective* Past; before the
time it is now: *The bus left five
minutes ago.*

196

**ag•o•ny** | **ăg′** ə nē | —*noun, plural*
**agonies** Great pain or suffering: *I broke my leg and was in agony.*

**aid** | ād | —*verb* **aided, aiding** To help or assist: *Carla will aid you in finding your new school.*

**aim** | ām | —*verb* **aimed, aiming** **1.** To point at something: *Aim the dart and then throw it at the target.*
**2.** To have a goal or purpose: *Judy and Shari aim to please their baseball coach.*

**air** | âr | —*noun* **1.** The mixture of gases surrounding the earth: *I opened the window to let in some air.* **2.** The space above the earth: *The air was full of brightly colored kites.*

**a•like** | ə **līk′** | —*adjective* Similar; like one another: *The goldfish in my fish tank all look alike.*

**al•most** | **ôl′** mōst′ | or | **ôl** mōst′ | —*adverb* Nearly: *It is almost time for lunch.*

**a•lone** | ə lōn′ | —*adjective* By oneself: *I like to walk by the sea all alone.*

**a•long** | ə **lông′** | or | ə **lŏng′** |
—*preposition* Beside the length of: *We walked along the beach.* —*adverb* Together; with someone: *When Jeff goes for a walk, his dog goes along.*

**always** | **ôl′** wāz | or | **ôl′** wĕz | —*adverb* At all times; every time: *Mollie always reads before she goes to bed.*

**a•pol•o•gize** | ə **pŏl′** ə jīz′ | —*verb* **apologized, apologizing** To say one is sorry: *I will apologize for being late to class.*

**ap•ple** | **ăp′** əl | —*noun, plural* **apples** A round fruit that is red, yellow, or green: *My favorite type of fruit pie is apple.*

**A•pril** | **ā′** prəl | —*noun* The fourth month of the year: *I play jokes on my brother every April Fool's Day.*

**arc•tic** | **ärk′** tĭk | or | **är′** tĭk | —*adjective* Very cold: *The arctic air froze the water in the lake.*

**aren't** | ärnt | or | **är′** ənt | The contraction of "are not": *Why aren't you coming to the playground with us?*

**arm** | ärm | —*noun, plural* **arms** The part of the body between the hand and the shoulder: *Zelda's arm hurt from pitching.*

**a•round** | ə **round′** | —*adverb* In a circle: *I watched the robin fly around.* —*preposition* About; here and there: *The circus traveled around the country.*

**art** | ärt | —*noun, plural* **arts** **1.** A painting, drawing, or sculpture. **2.** A skill or craft: *Dancing is an art.*

**ar•tis•tic** | är **tĭs′** tĭk | —*adjective* **1.** Having to do with art or artists: *The girls in the class have artistic interests.* **2.** Showing talent, skill, or good taste: *That is an artistic picture.*

**ask** | ăsk | or | äsk | —*verb* **asked, asking** **1.** To put a question to: *I asked my father where he was born.* **2.** To request: *I asked for a small pizza.*

**as•sure** | ə **shŏor′** | —*verb* **assured, assuring** **1.** To make sure or certain. **2.** To make less afraid: *My mother assured me that the dog would not bite.*

**ate** | āt | Look up **eat.** • **Ate** sounds like **eight.**

**ath•let•ic** | ăth **lĕt′** ĭk | —*adjective* **1.** Strong and active: *The athletic girl won every race.* **2.** Having to do with or for sports or athletes.

**at•tempt** | ə **tĕmpt′** | —*noun, plural* **attempts** A try or effort: *I made an attempt to draw a picture of my cat.*

**Au•gust** | **ô′** gəst | —*noun* The eighth month of the year: *The weather is always so hot in August.*

**197**

**buy** | bī | —*verb* **bought** | bôt | , **buying** To get by paying a price: *He bought a rocket model at the hobby shop. I'll buy popcorn at the hockey game.*
• **Buy** sounds like **by.**

**buz•zard** | **bŭz**′ ərd | —*noun, plural* **buzzards** A very large bird with a sharp, hooked beak and long, sharp claws; a vulture: *The buzzard was in the tree.*

**by** | bī | —*preposition* Beside or near to: *Leave your boots by the door.* • **By** sounds like **buy.**

# C

**ca•ble** | **kā**′ bəl | —*noun, plural* **cables** A strong thick rope often made of steel wire: *The boat is held to the dock by a cable.*

**came** | kām | Look up **come.**

**can** | kăn | or | kən | —*helping* or *auxiliary verb* Past tense **could** | kŏod | or | kəd | To be able to: *We could walk to the store if you're not too tired.*

**can't** | kănt | or | känt | The contraction of "cannot": *I can't stand wet feet.*

**card** | kärd | —*noun, plural* **cards** A small rectangular piece of cardboard or plastic: *Pen pals get cards from all over the world.*

**care** | kâr | —*noun, plural* **cares** Close attention: *The painter picked her colors with a lot of care.* —*verb* **cared, caring** To be concerned: *Millie cared what people thought about her.*

**care•less** | **kâr**′ lĭs | —*adjective* **1.** Not paying attention to what one is doing: *I fell off my bike because I was careless.* **2.** Done or made without care: *Lisa got a bad grade on her careless project.*

**carry** | **kăr**′ ē | —*verb* **carried, carrying, carries** To take from one place to another: *Will you help me carry these groceries home?*

**car•ton** | **kär**′ tn | —*noun, plural* **cartons** A container or box made of cardboard, paper, plastic, or other materials used for holding liquids or other objects: *We will recycle the egg carton.*

**cas•u•al** | **kăzh**′ ōo əl | —*adjective* Right for informal wear: *Sam wears casual clothes to school.*

**catch** | kăch | —*verb* **caught, catching** **1.** To get hold of; capture: *Billy tried to catch the cat.* **2.** To reach or get to in time: *I had to hurry to catch the train.*

**cav•ern** | **kăv**′ ərn | —*noun, plural* **caverns** A large cave: *Jim likes to explore caverns.*

**cel•e•bra•tion** | sĕl′ ə **brā**′ shən | —*noun, plural* **celebrations** A party or other activity carried on to honor a special occasion: *We had a celebration the last day of school.*

**cem•e•ter•y** | **sĕm**′ ĭ tĕr′ ē | —*noun, plural* **cemeteries** A place where dead people are buried: *The class put flowers on the graves in the cemetery.*

**cent** | sĕnt | —*noun, plural* **cents** A coin that is 1/100 of a dollar; a penny: *Bobby bought the notebook for 99 cents.* • **Cent** sounds like **sent.**

**chair** | châr | —*noun, plural* **chairs** A seat for one person, usually having four legs and a back: *The chair was so soft and comfortable, Joey fell asleep.*

**change** | chānj | —*verb,* **changed, changing 1.** To make different: *Leaves change color in the fall.* **2.** To replace; exchange: *I'll change this dress for a different one.*—*noun, plural* **changes** A thing that has become different: *The change in your homework is very good.*

**child** | chīld | —*noun, plural* **children** | **chĭl**′ drən | A young boy or girl: *Every child in the school went on the picnic. All children like fairy tales.*

**chil•dren** | **chĭl**′ drən | Look up **child.**

**chime** | chīm | —*noun, plural* **chimes**
1. A set of bells or pipes that make musical sounds. 2. A musical sound made by bells or a similar sound: *The chime of the doorbell woke me.*

**choice** | chois | —*noun, plural* **choices**
The power or chance to choose: *They had their choice of peanut butter sandwiches or tuna salad for lunch.*

**cir•cu•lar** | **sûr′** kyə lər | —*adjective*
Shaped like a circle; round: *The circular drawing was well done.*

**cit•y** | **sĭt′** ē | —*noun, plural* **cities** A large or important town: *Mom goes to the city every day to work.*

**clank** | klăngk | —*verb* **clanked, clanking**
To make a sound like two pieces of metal hitting each other: *The hammer clanked against the iron bell.*

**class** | klăs | or | kläs | —*noun, plural* **classes** A group of students taught by the same teacher or group of teachers: *Our class took a trip to the museum.*

**clock** | klŏk | —*noun, plural* **clocks** An instrument that tells time: *According to the kitchen clock, I was late again.*

**close** | klōs | —*adjective* **closer, closest** Near: *Sam is standing close to the door.* —*verb* | klōz | **closed, closing** To shut: *The suitcase was too full to close. I put the cookies in the oven and closed the door.*

**clown** | kloun | —*noun, plural* **clowns** A person who has a job in the circus or on stage making people laugh: *The clowns had big shoes and rubber noses.*

**coarse** | kôrs | —*adjective* **coarser, coarsest** 1. Made of large parts: *The sand on the beach was coarse.* 2. Rough: *Coarse wool makes me itch.*

**coat** | kōt | —*noun, plural* **coats** A piece of clothing worn over other clothes to keep warm: *Laura's new coat had a hood and a big zipper.*

**coax** | kōks | —*verb* **coaxed, coaxing** To try to persuade or convince by mild urging: *Jenny coaxed me to go to the dentist.*

**co•coa** | **kō′** kō′ | —*noun* A sweet drink made with cocoa and milk or water: *The best thing about ice-skating is drinking hot cocoa afterward.*

**coin** | koin | —*noun, plural* **coins** A piece of round, flat metal stamped by the government, used for money: *I had a lot of coins in my pocket.*

**comb** | kōm | —*noun, plural* **combs** A thin piece of hard material with teeth, used to arrange hair: *While Alice was untangling her hair, the comb broke.* —*verb* **combed, combing** 1. To arrange the hair: *I comb my dog's hair every day.* 2. To look thoroughly: *We combed the house for the missing watch.*

**come** | kŭm | —*verb* **came** | kām | , **coming** 1. To draw near; approach: *The lion came closer and closer to the mouse.* 2. To be available: *The toy robot came with two batteries.*

**com•ment** | **kŏm′** ĕnt′ | —*noun, plural* **comments** A remark or note that explains something or gives an opinion: *Jevon made a comment about the news.*

**con•sent** | kən **sent′** | —*verb* **consented, consenting** To agree to; to give permission: *Jim consented to clean his room once a week.*

**con•sole** | kən **sōl′** | —*verb* **consoled, consoling** To comfort: *When Kim's pet died, Sally consoled her.*

**201**

**con•tain** | kən **tān**′ | —*verb* **contained,
containing** To have in it; hold: *The
bowl contains soup.*

**cook** | koŏk | —*verb* **cooked, cooking** To
prepare food for eating by using
heat: *Cook the rice until it is fluffy.*

**cook•y** or **cook•ie** | koŏk′ ē | —*noun,
plural* **cookies** A small, flat, sweet
cake: *The cookies were shaped like
hearts.*

**cor•ner** | **kôr**′ nər | —*noun, plural*
**corners** The place where two lines or
sides meet: *My dog ate a corner of my
homework paper.*

**cor•ri•dor** | **kôr**′ ĭ dər | —*noun, plural*
**corridors** A long hall or passage in a
building: *The corridor in the hotel
was wide.*

**could** | koŏd | or | kəd | Look up **can.**

**couldn't** | **koŏd**′ nt | The contraction of
"could not": *We couldn't go to the
beach because it was raining.*

**could•ve** | **koŏd**′ əv | The contraction of
"could have": *Lisa could've gone to
the zoo, but she was sick.*

**count** | kount | —*noun, plural* **counts**
The number reached by counting: *A
count showed that one marble was
missing.* —*verb* **counted, counting**
To say numbers in order: *Fran's baby
sister can count to 20.*

**cov•er** | **kŭv**′ ər | —*verb* **covered,
covering** To put or lay over: *I covered
my bread with peanut butter.* —*noun,
plural* **covers** Something that is put
over another thing: *He hid the
present under the covers on his bed.*

**crin•kle** | **krĭng**′ kəl | —*verb* **crinkled,
crinkling** To wrinkle; crumple: *Betsy
crinkled the wrapping paper after she
opened the gift.*

**cry** | krī | —*verb* **cried, crying, cries** **1.** To
weep; shed tears: *Some people cry
when they are happy.* **2.** To shout or
call loudly: *If I need help, I'll cry out.*

**curl** | kûrl | —*verb* **curled, curling** To
twist into curves or coils: *The snake
curled around the rock.* —*noun,
plural* **curls** A coil of hair; a ringlet:
*She wore her hair in curls for the
party.*

**cy•cle** | **sī**′ kəl | —*noun, plural* **cycles**
**1.** A bicycle, tricycle, or motorcycle:
*My cycle is broken.* **2.** A series of
events that happen over and over in
the same order: *People enjoy the
cycle of seasons.*

# D

**dair•y** | **dâr**′ ē | —*noun, plural* **dairies** A
farm where cows are raised to
produce milk: *Our class took a field
trip to the dairy.*

**dan•ger** | **dān**′ jər | —*noun, plural*
**dangers** The chance of something
harmful happening: *A police officer
faces danger every day.*

**dark** | därk | —*adjective* **darker, darkest**
Having little or no light: *The cave
was very dark inside.* —*noun*
Nightfall: *The street lights come on
after dark.*

**daw•dle** | **dôd**′ l | —*verb* **dawdled,
dawdling** To take more time than
necessary: *I often dawdle on my way
home from school.*

**dear** | dîr | —*adjective* **dearer, dearest**
Loved: *Billy is a dear friend of mine.*
• **Dear** sounds like **deer.**

**de•bate** | dĭ **bāt**′ | —*verb* **debated,
debating** **1.** To think about in order
to decide: *I debated which book to
buy.* **2.** To discuss or argue reasons
for and against something.

**de•ceive** | dĭ **sēv**′ | —*verb* **deceived,
deceiving** To make a person believe
something that is not true; mislead:
*It was wrong to deceive my parents.*

**De•cem•ber** | dĭ **sěm**′ bər | —*noun* The
twelfth month of the year: *We are
going skiing in December.*

**deer** | dîr | —*noun, plural* **deer** A hoofed
animal that can run very fast: *Look
at the beautiful antlers on that male
deer.* • **Deer** sounds like **dear.**

**de•fine** | dǐ **fīn'** | —*verb* **defined, defining**
To give or explain the meaning of:
*Our teacher told us to define the spelling words.*

**de•pos•it** | dǐ **pŏz' ĭt** | —*verb* **deposited, depositing** 1. To put or place; set down: *I deposited my toys in the box.* 2. To put money in the bank.

**de•sign•er** | dǐ **zī' nər** | —*noun, plural* **designers** A person who makes the plan, pattern, or drawing for something: *The designer told us about her idea for a new doll.*

**des•sert** | dǐ **zûrt'** | —*noun, plural* **desserts** Food served last at a meal: *We had cake for dessert at the birthday party.*

**de•vour** | dǐ **vour'** | —*verb* **devoured, devouring** To eat in a hungry way: *The child will devour her lunch.*

**did•n't** | **dǐd' nt** | The contraction of "did not": *I didn't know who you were.*

**dirt** | dûrt | —*noun* Loose earth or soil: *He drew a map in the dirt with a stick.*

**dirt•y** | **dûr' tē** | —*adjective* **dirtier, dirtiest** Not clean: *I stepped in the mud and got my shoes dirty.*

**dish** | dǐsh | —*noun, plural* **dishes** 1. A plate or bowl used for holding food: *The clown balanced a dish on his nose.* 2. A particular food: *Barbara's favorite dish was spaghetti.*

**dis•may** | dǐs **mā'** | —*noun* A feeling of fear or loss of courage when danger or trouble comes: *I felt dismay when my rabbit got out of its pen.*

**dis•pute** | dǐ **spyoot'** | —*noun, plural* **disputes** An argument or quarrel: *My friend and I had a dispute.*

**do** | doo | —*verb* **did, done** | dun | , **doing, does** | duz | 1. To perform; complete: *Bibi, the circus monkey, is always doing things that make people laugh.* 2. To be good enough: *No one had done as well on the test as Valerie.* —*helping* or *auxiliary verb* **Do** is used to ask questions: *Does she swim?*

**does** | dŭz | Look up **do.**

**dome** | dōm | —*noun, plural* **domes** A round roof or top that looks like half of a ball: *The building for the football games has a dome.*

**done** | dŭn | Look up **do.**

**don't** | dōnt | The contraction of "do not": *Don't sit on that wet bench.*

**door** | dôr | or | dōr | —*noun, plural* **doors** 1. A movable panel that swings or slides to open or close the entrance to a room, building, or vehicle: *Jill slammed the door behind her.* 2. A doorway: *Marta walked through the door.*

**doubt•ful** | **dout' fəl** | —*adjective* Feeling, showing, or causing uncertainty; not sure: *Kim was doubtful that she could stay awake all night.*

**down¹** | doun | —*adverb* From a higher to a lower point on: *The ball rolled down the hill.*

**down²** | doun | —*noun* The soft under feathers of birds: *Sandy's new ski jacket was filled with down.*

**draw** | drô | —*verb* **drew, drawn, drawing** To make a picture with pen, pencil, crayon, etc.: *I can draw great pictures of airplanes.*

**dream** | drēm | —*noun, plural* **dreams** Something felt, thought, or seen during sleep: *I had a dream about a giant bee.* —*verb* **dreamed** or **dreamt, dreaming** To think, feel, or see during sleep; have dreams: *Amy dreamed that she could fly.*

**drear•y** | **drîr' ē** | —*adjective* **drearier, dreariest** Sad; gloomy: *The rainy day was dreary.*

203

**dress** | drĕs | —*noun, plural* **dresses** A piece of clothing worn by women and girls, usually having a top and skirt made in one piece: *Mary bought a new dress for the class party.* —*verb* **dressed, dressing** To put clothes on: *Get dressed and we'll go shopping.*

**drive** | drīv | —*verb* **drove, driven, driving** 1. To steer a vehicle: *Drive the car carefully.* 2. To carry in a vehicle: *My mom promised to drive me to the rodeo.* —*noun, plural* **drives** A ride in a vehicle: *Let's go for a drive in the country.*

**drop** | drŏp | —*verb* **dropped, dropping** To fall or let fall: *The pan was so hot, he dropped it. The soap was so slippery, Barbara kept dropping it.*

# E

**each** | ēch | —*adjective* Every one of: *Each student in the class gave me a report.*

**ear** | îr | —*noun, plural* **ears** 1. The part of the body with which animals and people hear: *An elephant's ears are big and floppy.* 2. Attention: *This message is important so give me your ear.*

**earth** | ûrth | —*noun* 1. The planet on which human beings live: *The earth is the third planet from the sun.* 2. Soil; ground: *We planted a tree in the earth.*

**eat** | ēt | —*verb* **ate** | āt |, **eaten, eating** To take meals: *I ate dinner at my best friend's house.*

**egg** | ĕg | —*noun, plural* **eggs** The contents of a chicken egg, used as food: *I like to crack the shells of eggs.*

**eight** | āt | —*adjective* Being one more than seven in number: *An octopus has eight tentacles.* • **Eight** sounds like **ate.**

**end** | ĕnd | —*noun, plural* **ends** The finish of a thing: *The road comes to an end at the river.* —*verb* **ended, ending** To finish; to bring to an end: *The concert ended with a fireworks show.*

**end•ing** | ĕn′ ding | —*noun, plural* **endings** The last part: *The movie had a scary ending, so I closed my eyes.*

**en•dure** | ĕn dŏor′ | or | ĕn dyŏor′ | —*verb* **endured, enduring** 1. To put up with: *The campers had to endure cold weather.* 2. To continue; last. *The pyramids have endured a long time.*

**en•joy** | ĕn joi′ | —*verb* **enjoyed, enjoying** To like to do: *I enjoy singing along with the radio.*

**en•joy•ment** | ĕn joi′ mənt | —*noun, plural* **enjoyments** Joy; pleasure: *We get enjoyment from a good book.*

**es•ti•mate** | ĕs′ tə māt′ | —*verb* **estimated, estimating** To guess by thinking about clearly: *We estimated that the trip would take five hours.*

**e•ven** | ē′ vən | —*adjective* Smooth; flat: *Willy likes to ride his bike on this road because it's so even.* —*adverb* 1. As well as: *The boys were all dressed up, even Mitch.* 2. In spite of: *I'll go horseback riding with you even though I don't like horses.*

**eve•ry** | ĕv′ rē | —*adjective* All in an entire group; each one: *Lou read every mystery book in the library.*

**eye** | ī | —*noun, plural* **eyes** 1. One of two round organs with which a person or animal sees: *My eyes followed the home run right out of the field.* 2. A close watch: *Please keep an eye on my bike.*

# F

**fa•ble** | fā′ bəl | —*noun, plural* **fables** A story that teaches a lesson: *My favorite fable is about the lion and the mouse.*

**face** | fās | —*noun, plural* **faces** The front of the head: *Murray had spots on his face from the measles.*

**fal•ter** | fôl′ tər | —*verb* **faltered, faltering** To act, speak, or move in an unsteady way: *My voice was faltering when I gave my speech.*

**fam•i•ly** | făm′ ə lē | *or* | făm′ lē | —*noun, plural* **families** Parents and their children: *My family always goes on vacation together.*

**fa•ther** | fä′ thər | —*noun, plural* **fathers** The male parent of a child: *Betty's father took her to the doctor today.*

**feat** | fēt | —*noun, plural* **feats** An act or deed that shows great bravery, skill, or strength: *Riding the bicycle ten miles was a feat.*

**Feb•ru•ar•y** | fĕb′ rōō ĕr′ ē | *or* | fĕb′ yōō ĕr′ ē | —*noun* The second month of the year: *Ground-Hog Day comes in February.*

**few** | fyōō | —*adjective* **fewer, fewest** Not many: *There were only a few peanuts left in the bag. There are fewer cookies here than there were a minute ago.*

**fill** | fĭl | —*verb* **filled, filling** **1.** To make or become full: *I always fill the sugar bowl to the top.* **2.** To spread throughout: *My writing filled the pages of my diary.*

**find** | fīnd | —*verb* **found** | found | , **finding 1.** To look for and get back: *I found my keys under my bed.* **2.** To look for and discover: *Polar bears are only found in the Far North.*

**fire** | fīr | —*noun, plural* **fires** Heat and light given off by burning something: *They saw the fire and ran for help.*

**first** | fûrst | —*adjective* Coming before any other in time, place, or order: *This is my first pair of ice skates.* —*noun* Person or thing that is first: *Mark was first in line.*

   *Idiom.* **at first.** In the beginning: *Ellen didn't want to go swimming at first, but she changed her mind.*

**floor** | flôr | *or* | flōr | —*noun, plural* **floors** The part of a room people walk on: *The floor squeaks when you walk on it.*

**flour•ish** | flûr′ ĭsh | —*verb* **flourished, flourishing** To grow strongly and well: *The flowers flourish in the sunny garden.*

**flow•er** | flou′ ər | —*noun, plural* **flowers** The part of the plant where seeds are made; the blossom: *This plant has yellow flowers.*

**fly** | flī | —*verb* **flew, flown, flying, flies** To move through the air with wings: *I love to watch airplanes fly in and out of the airport.*

**foot** | fŏŏt | —*noun, plural* **feet** The part of the leg on which a person or animal walks: *I put my shoe on the wrong foot.*

**for•get** | fər gĕt′ | —*verb* **forgot** | fər gŏt′ | , **forgotten** To be unable to remember: *Don't forget to study for your math test. I forgot to study for the test.*

**for•got** | fər gŏt′ | Look up **forget.**

**fork** | fôrk | —*noun, plural* **forks 1.** A tool used to pick up food: *I like to eat spaghetti with my fingers, but Mom makes me use a fork.* **2.** A place where something divides into more than one part: *When we came to the fork in the trail, we didn't know which way to go.*

**found** | found | Look up **find.**

**four** | fôr | *or* | fōr | —*noun* The number that follows three: *Two plus two is four.* —*adjective* Being one more than three in number: *There are four people in my family.*

**frag•ile** | frăj′ əl | —*adjective* Easy to break or damage: *The glass is fragile.*

205

**frail** | frāl | —*adjective* **frailer, frailest**
1. Easily broken or damaged: *The very old chair is frail.* 2. Not having strength; weak: *I was frail after my illness.*

**free** | frē | —*adjective* **freer, freest** 1. Not under someone else's control: *The cat was free to roam around the neighborhood.* 2. Without cost: *We won free tickets to the show.*

**Fri•day** | **frī**′ dē | or | **frī**′ dā′ | —*noun, plural* **Fridays** The sixth day of the week: *We don't get homework on Friday.*

**friend** | frĕnd | —*noun, plural* **friends** A person one knows and likes: *My friend and I write letters to each other in a secret code.*

**friend•li•ness** | **frĕnd**′ lē nəs | —*noun* The manner or actions of a friend: *Aaron's friendliness makes everyone feel welcome.*

**frog** | frôg | or | frŏg | —*noun, plural* **frogs** A small animal with webbed feet and smooth skin: *Frogs use their long sticky tongues to catch insects.*

**from** | frŭm | or | frŏm | or | frəm | —*preposition* 1. Having as a place of origin: *I got a letter from my cousin.* 2. Starting at: *The boys raced from school to their house.*

**front** | frŭnt | —*noun, plural* **fronts** The part of something that faces forward: *There was a crowd in front of the record store.*

**fron•tier** | frŭn tîr′ | —*noun, plural* **frontiers** 1. The border between countries: *The family crossed the frontier between Mexico and the United States.* 2. The far edge of a country where people are just beginning to live.

**ful•fill** | fŏŏl fĭl′ | —*verb* **fulfilled, fulfilling** To carry out, finish, or do what is called for: *Amy fulfilled her promise to walk the dog every day.*

**full** | fŏŏl | —*adjective* **fuller, fullest** Holding all that it can hold: *My stomach was full after dinner.*

**fun•ny** | **fŭn**′ ē | —*adjective* **funnier, funniest** Causing laughter; amusing: *Sammy's jokes are very funny. Brad's jokes are always funnier than mine.*

**fur** | fûr | —*noun, plural* **furs** Thick, soft hair that covers certain animals: *My dog's fur keeps him warm in the winter.*

# G

**gar•den** | **gär**′ dn | —*noun, plural* **gardens** A piece of land used for growing vegetables and flowers: *We planted tomatoes and lettuce in the garden.*

**gen•u•ine** | **jĕn**′ yŏŏ ĭn | —*adjective* 1. Real: *The genuine ruby costs a lot of money.* 2. Sincere; honest: *My aunt showed a genuine interest in my story.*

**girl** | gûrl | —*noun, plural* **girls** A female child: *Barbi was the only girl on the team.*

**glid•er** | **glī**′ dər | —*noun, plural* **gliders** An aircraft that flies without a motor and moves easily on currents of air: *The ride in the glider was fun.*

**go** | gō | —*verb* **goes** | gōz | , **went, gone, going** To move; travel: *Mary goes to the dentist every year.*

**goes** | gōz | Look up **go.**

**gold** | gōld | —*noun* A heavy, precious, yellow metal used for making jewelry and coins: *James has a piece of gold that belonged to his grandfather.*

**gour•met** | gŏŏr mā′ | or | **gŏŏr**′ mā′ | —*noun, plural* **gourmets** A person who loves fine food and knows a great deal about it. **Gourmet** is often used to modify another noun: *Mother cooked a gourmet dinner.*

**gov•ern** | **gŭv**′ ərn | —*verb* **governed, governing** To rule, control, direct, or manage: *The king governed the country for ten years.*

**gray** | grā | —*noun, plural* **grays** Any color that is a mixture of black and white: *Do you like the color gray?* —*adjective* **grayer, grayest** Having the color gray: *I have a gray cat.*

**great** | grāt | —*adjective* **greater, greatest** Wonderful; very good: *It would be great to travel around the world. This is the greatest zoo I've ever seen.*

**ground** | ground | —*noun* Soil; land: *The ground was covered with snow after the storm.*

**guess** | gĕs | —*verb* **guessed, guessing** **1.** To form an opinion without enough knowledge: *Let's try guessing what the surprise will be.* **2.** To think; suppose: *I guess I'll just stay here.*

# H

**had•n't** | hăd′ nt | The contraction of "had not": *I hadn't known him long before he moved away.*

**hair** | hâr | —*noun, plural* **hairs** The thin, threadlike strands that grow from a person's or animal's skin: *Nan wears her long hair in a braid.*

**half** | hăf | or | häf | —*noun, plural* **halves** One of two equal parts: *Jean ate half of her sandwich, and I ate the other half.*

**ham•mer** | hăm′ ər | —*noun, plural* **hammers** A tool with an iron head used to drive in nails: *I need a hammer to put the birdhouse together.*

**hand** | hănd | —*noun, plural* **hands** The part of the arm below the wrist: *I held the baby chick in my hands.* —*verb* **handed, handing** To pass with the hands: *I handed the teacher my story.*

**hap•py** | hăp′ ē | —*adjective* **happier, happiest** Feeling pleased or joyful: *She was happy when she won the award.*

**hard** | härd | —*adjective* **harder, hardest** Not easy: *This math test is too hard.* —*adverb* **harder, hardest** With energy or effort: *Biff worked hard.*

**has•n't** | hăz′ ənt | The contraction of "has not": *Joey hasn't gone yet.*

**have•n't** | hăv′ ənt | The contraction of "have not": *I haven't heard from Dolly since she went to camp.*

**head** | hĕd | —*noun, plural* **heads** The top part of the body that contains the brain, eyes, ears, nose, and mouth: *Jane put the hat on her head.* —*verb* **headed, heading** To go toward: *The bird headed south for the winter.*

**hear** | hîr | —*verb* **heard, hearing** **1.** To be aware of sound: *Do you hear a noise in the attic?* **2.** To be told: *Emily and her class were about to hear the story of Daniel Boone.*
• **Hear** sounds like **here.**

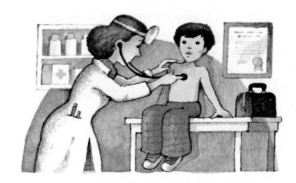

**heart** | härt | —*noun, plural* **hearts** **1.** The organ in the chest that pumps blood through the body: *The doctor listened to my heart.* **2.** Courage and enthusiasm: *Howard put his whole heart into winning the game.*

**hel•lo** | hĕ lō′ | or | hə lō′ | or | hĕl′ ō | —*interjection* A greeting: *Sharon always answers the phone with a cheery "Hello."*

**help** | hĕlp | —*verb* **helped, helping** To aid or assist; to be useful: *Will you help me hang this picture? I helped Dee buy new jeans.*

207

**here** | hîr | —*adverb* In this place or spot: *Cheri and I have been waiting here all afternoon.* —*noun* This place: *The ice cream truck is four blocks from here.* • **Here** sounds like **hear.**

**he's** | hēz | The contraction of "he is": *He's the new president of the photography club.*

**high** | hī | **higher, highest** —*adjective* Tall: *That pine tree is 25 feet high.* —*adverb* At or to a high point: *My balloon flew high up in the sky.*

**hold** | hōld | —*verb* **held, holding** **1.** To have and keep in the hand; grasp: *I have to hold my sister's hand when we go shopping.* **2.** To keep in a certain position: *Hold your head still while I comb your hair.*

**hole** | hōl | —*noun, plural* **holes** A hollow or empty place in something solid: *The pirates dug a hole and buried a treasure chest.* • **Hole** sounds like **whole.**

**hope** | hōp | —*verb* **hoped, hoping** To wish for something: *I hope my grandmother feels better soon. Julia hoped she wouldn't be late for school.*

**hot** | hŏt | —*adjective* **hotter, hottest** Very warm: *It is hotter outside today than it was yesterday.*

**hour** | our | —*noun, plural* **hours** A period of time equal to 60 minutes: *The bread will take one hour to bake.* • **Hour** sounds like **our.**

**house** | hous | —*noun, plural* **houses** | **hou**′ zĭz | A building that people live in: *The Scouts met at my house.*

**how'd** | houd | The contraction of "how did": *How'd you tie the knot?*

**hud•dle** | hŭd′ l | —*noun, plural* **huddles** A group or crowd that is closely gathered or packed together: *Our team plans the next play when we are in a huddle.* —*verb* **huddled, huddling** To gather close together: *The campers huddled in the tent.*

**hun•dred** | hŭn′ drĭd | —*noun, plural* **hundreds** The number that follows 99: *Fifty plus fifty is one hundred.* —*adjective* Being one more than 99 in number: *There are 100 pages in this book.*

# I

**I'd** | īd | The contraction of "I had," "I would," or "I should": *I'd better get home before dark. I'd rather eat brownies than bake them.*

**I'll** | īl | The contraction of "I will" or "I shall": *I'll never remember everyone's name.*

**I'm** | īm | The contraction of "I am": *I'm sure I will make the team.*

**in•come** | ĭn′ kŭm′ | —*noun, plural* **incomes** Money that a person receives for work or from other things during a certain period of time: *Tim wants to earn an income as a teacher.*

**in•dex** | ĭn′ dĕks′ | —*noun, plural* **indexes** An alphabetical list of names and subjects at the end of a book that gives the page or pages where each can be found: *Mary looked in the index to find the pages where butterflies are described.*

**in•side** | ĭn′ sīd′ | or | ĭn **sīd**′ | —*noun, plural* **insides** The inner part: *We painted the inside of the house.* —*preposition* | ĭn **sīd**′ | Into: *She put her hand inside the grab bag and pulled out a whistle.*

**in•spire** | ĭn **spīr**′ | —*verb* **inspired, inspiring** **1.** To move the mind, feelings, or imagination: *Nature may inspire the artist.* **2.** To move to action: *Since I had a solo, I was inspired to practice.*

**in•stall** | ĭn **stôl**′ | —*verb* **installed, installing** To put in place for use or service: *My father will install a new furnace.*

**in•struct** | ĭn **strŭkt**′ | —*verb* **instructed, instructing** To teach or show how to do something: *Will Bruce instruct the tennis class?*

**is•n't** | ĭz′ ənt | The contraction of "is not": *This isn't my lunch box.*

**it's** | ĭts | The contraction of "it is" or "it has": *It's time for lunch. It's been a long time since I saw my aunt.*

**I've** | īv | The contraction of "I have": *I've never seen a movie that scared me as much as this one.*

## J

**jab** | jăb | —*verb* **jabbed, jabbing** To poke with something pointed: *Please stop jabbing me with your finger.*

**Jan•u•ar•y** | jăn′ yōō ĕr′ ē | —*noun* The first month of the year: *January has 31 days.*

**jog** | jŏg | —*verb* **jogged, jogging** To run slowly: *My mom jogged two miles this morning.*

**join** | join | —*verb* **joined, joining** **1.** To put together: *We joined hands and made a circle.* **2.** To take part with others: *Will you join us for a swim across the lake?*

**joke** | jōk | —*noun, plural* **jokes** Something funny said or done to make someone laugh: *Steve makes everyone laugh with his elephant jokes.* —*verb* **joked, joking** To do or say something as a joke: *I was only joking.*

**joy** | joi | —*noun, plural* **joys** A feeling of great happiness: *My dog jumps for joy when he sees me.*

**Ju•ly** | jōō lī′ | —*noun* The seventh month of the year: *Are you going on a vacation in July?*

**June** | jōōn | —*noun* The sixth month of the year: *School is over in June.*

**just** | jŭst | —*adjective* Fair: *Tim didn't think the teacher was just in giving a surprise test.* —*adverb* At that moment: *Just when he fell asleep the phone rang.*

## K

**keep** | kēp | —*verb* **kept, keeping** **1.** To have; own: *You may keep the picture.* **2.** To continue in a certain condition or place; to stay: *I kept the hamster in a cage.*

**key** | kē | —*noun, plural* **keys** **1.** A piece of shaped metal used to open a lock: *I lost my key, so I couldn't get in the house.* **2.** The most important part: *Exercise is a key to good health.*

**kick** | kĭk | —*verb* **kicked, kicking** To hit with the foot: *I saw the horse kick a hole in the barn door.*

**kind¹** | kīnd | —*adjective* **kinder, kindest** Thoughtful; helpful: *The nurse is a very kind person.*

**kind²** | kīnd | —*noun, plural* **kinds** A type; variety: *What kind of music do you like?*

**knew** | nōō | or | nyōō | Look up **know.**

**know** | nō | —*verb* **knew** | nōō | or | nyōō | , **known, knowing** **1.** To be certain of the facts: *I know you are hiding under the stairs.* **2.** To be familiar with: *Penny knew everyone in school.*

## L

**la•bor** | lā′ bər | —*noun, plural* **labors** Hard work: *Making a new garden took much labor.* —*verb* **labored, laboring** To work hard: *Jacob labored to do the math problem.*

**late** | lāt | —*adverb* **later, latest** After the usual or expected time: *The school bus was waiting because I was late. John was even later today than usual.*

**laugh** | lăf | or | läf | —*verb* **laughed, laughing** To make sounds and move your face to show joy or amusement: *I couldn't help laughing at his hat.*

**lead** | lēd | —*verb* **led** | lĕd | , **leading** To show the way: *The guide at the park led the way.*

**learn** | lûrn | —*verb* **learned** or **learnt, learning** To gain knowledge or skill: *Erma wants to learn how to speak Spanish.*

**light¹** | līt | —*noun, plural* **lights** Anything that gives off the energy by which we see, such as a lamp: *Turn off the light before you go to sleep.*

**light²** | līt | —*adjective* **lighter, lightest** Not heavy: *The box was light because it was empty.*

**like¹** | līk | —*verb* **liked, liking 1.** To be fond of someone or something: *I have always liked my cousin, Sal.* **2.** To enjoy: *Ida liked to dance.*

**like²** | līk | —*preposition.* **1.** Similar to: *Harriet's coat is just like mine.* **2.** In the mood for: *I feel like going for a walk.*

**line** | līn | —*noun, plural* **lines** A long row of people or things: *He stood in line for hours to get carnival tickets.*

**li•on** | lī′ ən | —*noun, plural* **lions** A large, wild cat from Africa or Asia: *Only male lions have manes.*

**lit•tle** | lĭt′ l | —*adjective* **littler, littlest,** or **least** Small in size or quantity: *My kitten is still very little.*

**loaf¹** | lōf | —*noun, plural* **loaves** Bread baked in one piece or shape: *I sliced the loaf of bread that I'd just made.*

**loaf²** | lōf | —*verb* **loafed, loafing** To be lazy: *My dog loafs around the house.*

**long** | lông | or | lŏng | —*adjective* **longer, longest** Not short; great in length or time: *The school play was very long. That is the longest snake I have ever seen.* —*adverb* **longer, longest** For a great amount of time: *Take as long as you need to finish the test.*

**loss** | lôs | —*noun, plural* **losses** The act or fact of not winning something: *Our hockey team has ten losses.*

**love•ly** | lŭv′ lē | —*adjective* **lovelier, loveliest** Beautiful: *The flowers look lovely on the table.*

**lug•gage** | lŭg′ ĭj | —*noun* Suitcases and bags that a person takes on a trip: *We were told not to take too much luggage on our trip.*

**lunch** | lŭnch | —*noun, plural* **lunches** The midday meal: *Ethan always has a sandwich for lunch.*

# M

**main•tain** | mān tān′ | —*verb* **maintained, maintaining 1.** To keep in good condition: *Mark will help maintain the garden.* **2.** To continue to have; keep.

**mall** | môl | or | măl | —*noun, plural* **malls** A shopping center: *Mom took me to the mall to buy some new clothes.*

**man•y** | mĕn′ ē | —*adjective* **more, most** A large number of: *Many animals live in this forest.*

**March** | märch | —*noun* The third month of the year: *March is the best month for flying kites.*

**mar•ket** | mär′ kĭt | —*noun, plural* **markets** A place where goods are bought and sold: *We always go to the market for fresh vegetables.*

**match¹** | măch | —*verb* **matched, matching**  To be alike; to look alike: *These two socks match.*

**match²** | măch | —*noun, plural* **matches**  A small stick of wood or cardboard that bursts into flame when rubbed: *Always keep your matches in a dry place when you are camping.*

**mat•ter** | **măt**′ ər | —*noun, plural* **matters**  Problem or trouble: *What's the matter with your goldfish? —verb* **mattered, mattering**  To be of importance: *Does it matter to you if we go to the store first?*

**May** | mā | —*noun*  The fifth month of the year: *My family always gives a picnic on Memorial Day in May.*

**meat** | mēt | —*noun*  The flesh of animals used as food: *We had meat and salad for dinner.* • **Meat** sounds like **meet.**

**meet** | mēt | —*verb* **met, meeting**  To come together; come face to face: *Meet me on the corner after school. The club is meeting this afternoon.* • **Meet** sounds like **meat.**

**meet•ing** | **mē**′ tĭng | —*noun, plural* **meetings**  A coming together for some common purpose: *The lion called a meeting of all the animals in his kingdom.*

**me•te•or** | **mē**′ tē ər | —*noun, plural* **meteors**  Matter from space that forms a bright trail or streak of light as it burns when it enters the earth's atmosphere: *We saw two meteors last night.*

**mile** | mīl | —*noun, plural* **miles**  A unit of distance equal to 5,280 feet or 1,609.34 meters: *The baseball field is two miles away from my house.*

**mind** | mīnd | —*noun, plural* **minds**  The part of a person that thinks, feels, learns, etc.: *He has a good mind, if only he would use it. —verb* **minded, minding**  To object to: *Would you mind if I borrowed your record?*

**mine** | mīn | —*pronoun*  The thing or things belonging to me: *That's Bobby's bed, and this one is mine.*

**mis•er•y** | **mĭz**′ ə rē | —*noun, plural* **miseries**  Great pain or unhappiness: *The tornado caused misery for anyone in its path.*

**moist•en** | **moi**′ sən | —*verb* **moistened, moistening**  To make slightly wet or damp: *The rain moistened the garden.*

**Mon•day** | **mŭn**′ dē | or | **mŭn**′ dā′ | —*noun*  The second day of the week: *Sometimes it's hard to wake up on Monday.*

**mon•ey** | **mŭn**′ ē | —*noun*  Coins and bills printed by a government and used to pay for things: *Judy is saving her money to buy a radio.*

**month** | mŭnth | —*noun*  One of 12 parts the year is divided into: *My birthday is this month.*

**morn•ing** | **môr**′ nĭng | —*noun, plural* **mornings**  The early part of the day: *I have cereal for breakfast every morning.*

**most** | mōst | —*adjective*  The greatest amount: *The team that gets the most runs will win. —noun*  The larger part: *I like most of the people in this club.*

**moth•er** | **mŭth**′ ər | —*noun, plural* **mothers**  A female parent of a child: *Marty's mother writes articles for magazines.*

**move** | mōōv | —*verb* **moved, moving**  To change from one position to another: *Mom is always moving the furniture around. —noun, plural* **moves**  The act of moving: *The frog made his move and caught the fly.*

**much** | mŭch | **more, most** —*adjective*  Great in amount: *I have much work to do. —adverb*  Greatly; to a large degree: *Frank is much excited about his award.*

**must** | mŭst | —*helping* or *auxiliary verb*  Will have to; should: *You must wear a smock in art class.*

**must•n't** | **mŭs**′ ənt |  The contraction of "must not": *Carl mustn't have heard the dinner bell.*

# N

**near** | nîr | —*adverb* **nearer, nearest** Not far from; close to: *Randy lives near his grandparents.*

**neck•tie** | **nĕk**′ tī′ | —*noun, plural* **neckties** A band of cloth worn around the neck and tied in a knot in front: *Nick likes to give his father neckties for gifts.*

**need** | nēd | —*verb* **needed, needing** To require; must have: *I need a whistle to call my dog.*

**nev•er** | **nĕv**′ ər | —*adverb* Not at any time: *Ben never gives up.*

**news** | no͞oz | or | nyo͞oz | —*noun* (Used with a singular verb.) Recent events or information: *The news about the science fair is good.*

**next** | nĕkst | —*adjective* **1.** Coming right after: *We'll get on the next car of the roller coaster.* **2.** Nearest in position: *Chuck lives in the next apartment.*

**nice** | nīs | —*adjective* **nicer, nicest** Pleasant; agreeable: *It was a nice evening for a walk.*

**night** | nīt | —*noun, plural* **nights** The time between sunset and sunrise: *On a clear night, it's fun to look at the stars.*

**noise** | noiz | —*noun, plural* **noises** A sound, especially if loud: *The crying baby made a lot of noise.*

**none** | nŭn | —*pronoun* Not any; not one: *None of my friends can ski.*

**noon** | no͞on | —*noun* Midday; 12 o'clock in the middle of the day: *Walter went home at noon for lunch.*

**north** | nôrth | —*noun* The direction toward the North Pole: *A compass needle always points the way north.* —*adverb* Toward the north: *Bobby walked north to go into town.*

**noth•ing** | **nŭth**′ ĭng | —*pronoun* **1.** Not anything: *Nothing the clown did made the child smile.* **2.** Of no importance: *It's nothing at all.* **3.** Zero: *The score was one to nothing.*

**No•vem•ber** | nō **vĕm**′ bər | —*noun* The eleventh month of the year: *We eat turkey in November.*

**num•ber** | **nŭm**′ bər | —*noun, plural* **numbers** **1.** A figure or numeral that identifies something: *His football number is 12.* **2.** Amount: *Tell me the number of marbles you have.*

# O

**o'clock** | ə **klŏk**′ | —*adverb* According to the clock: *My favorite TV show begins at 7 o'clock.*

**Oc•to•ber** | ôk **tō**′ bər | —*noun* The tenth month of the year: *Halloween is the last day of October.*

**off** | ôf | or | ŏf | —*adjective* Not on; removed: *He worked with his shirt off.* —*preposition* Away from a place: *She dived off the pier.*

**oil** | oil | —*noun* **1.** A greasy liquid or fat that easily becomes liquid: *We dropped the popcorn into the hot oil.* **2.** Petroleum: *They drill for oil.*

**one** | wŭn | —*noun* A number, written 1: *One plus two equals three.* —*pronoun* A particular person or thing: *One of my turtles is missing.* • **One** sounds like **won.**

**on•ly** | **ōn**′ lē | —*adjective* Sole; without others: *This is my only brother, Harold.* —*adverb* Just; merely: *Phil was 14, but he acted as if he were only 4.*

**o•pen** | **ō**′ pən | —*verb* **opened, opening** To cause something to be no longer closed: *I couldn't wait to open the box that was for me.*

**or•na•ment** | **ôr**′ nə mənt | —*noun, plural* **ornaments** An object that makes something more beautiful: *The ornament is blue and red.*

**oth•er** | **ŭth**′ ər | —*adjective* Different: *I have other things to do.* —*noun, plural* **others** The remaining people or things: *Mom carried the big box and I carried all the others.*

**our** | our | —*pronoun* Of or belonging to us: *Our dog followed us to school.*
• **Our** sounds like **hour.**

**o•ver** | ō′ vər | —*preposition* **1.** Above; higher than: *It was raining, but at least we had a tent over our heads.* **2.** On top of; upon: *Teddy spilled raisins all over the floor.* —*adjective* Finished: *The play is over.*

**owl** | oul | —*noun, plural* **owls** A kind of bird with a flat face, large eyes, and a short, hooked beak. Owls make a hooting sound: *The hoot of the owl scares some people.*

**own** | ōn | —*verb* **owned, owning** To have; possess: *Do you own the dog that is following you?*

# P

**page¹** | pāj | —*noun, plural* **pages** One side of a leaf of paper in a book: *For homework I had to read pages 17 and 18 in my science book.*

**page²** | pāj | —*noun, plural* **pages** A person who runs errands or delivers messages: *The page carried my message to my hotel room.* —*verb* **paged, paging** To call for someone in a public place: *When Tom got lost in the airport, his mother paged him on the loudspeaker.*

**paint** | pānt | —*noun, plural* **paints** Coloring matter mixed with oil or water: *John made a picture with 12*

different colors of paint. —*verb* **painted, painting** **1.** To cover or coat something with paint: *Alice painted her skateboard blue.* **2.** To make a picture using paint: *He liked to paint pictures of his dog, Igor.*

**pa•per** | pā′ pər | —*noun, plural* **papers** **1.** Material made from wood pulp, rags, etc. Paper is usually in the form of thin sheets. It is used for writing, drawing, printing, wrapping packages, and covering walls: *Tony used up all the paper in the house writing letters to his pen pal.* **2.** A newspaper: *I read about the parade in the paper.*

**pa•trol** | pə trōl′ | —*noun, plural* **patrols** A person or group of people who move about an area to make sure everything is all right: *The patrol looked for snakes.*

**pay** | pā | —*verb,* **paid, paying** **1.** To give money for something bought or for work done: *I had to pay 50 dollars for my new bicycle.* **2.** To give, or make, or do: *I always pay attention in dance class.* —*noun* Money given for work done: *My pay for raking the leaves was one dollar.*

**pen•ny** | pĕn′ ē | —*noun, plural* **pennies** One cent: *When I've saved 100 pennies, I'll have one dollar.*

**peo•ple** | pē′ pəl | —*noun, plural* **people** Human beings: *There were a lot of people at the party.*

**place** | plās | —*noun, plural* **places** A particular spot: *People travel from many places to see the rodeo.* —*verb* **placed, placing** To put in a particular spot or position: *I placed the toys on the shelf.*

   *Idiom.* **take place.** To happen: *I like to watch the fireworks take place on the Fourth of July.*

**plaid** | plăd | *noun, plural* **plaids** A design of stripes of different widths and colors that cross each other to make squares: *Megan has a plaid dress.*

**please** | plēz | —*verb* **pleased, pleasing**
**1.** To give pleasure or happiness to; to be agreeable to: *He was pleased when I took him to the circus.* **2.** Be so kind as to: *Please close the door.*

**point** | point | —*noun, plural* **points**
Sharp or narrowed end of something; the tip: *I broke the point on my pencil.* —*verb* **pointed, pointing** To call attention to with the finger; to show.

**poi•son•ous** | **poi**′ zə nəs | —*adjective*
Having poison in it or having the effects of poison: *We were careful not to step on a poisonous snake.*

**poor** | pŏor | —*adjective* **poorer, poorest**
**1.** Having little or no money: *She was too poor to go to the movies with her friends.* **2.** Needing pity: *The poor little mouse was afraid of the big cat.*

**pop•corn** | **pŏp**′ kôrn′ | —*noun* A kind of corn that pops open and puffs up when heated: *I like watching popcorn pop almost as much as I like eating it.*

**pour** | pôr | or | pōr | —*verb* **poured, pouring 1.** To cause to flow in a stream: *I always pour maple syrup over my pancakes.* **2.** A heavy rain: *We put up our umbrellas as it started to pour.*

**pow•er** | **pou**′ ər | —*noun, plural* **powers**
Strength or force: *A runner has plenty of power in her legs.*

**pret•ty** | **prĭt**′ ē | —*adjective* **prettier, prettiest** Pleasing; attractive; appealing: *The sunset was very pretty. That is the prettiest flower I ever saw.*

**prob•lem** | **prŏb**′ ləm | —*noun, plural* **problems** A question that is hard to understand or settle: *Matt's problem was that his little sister followed him wherever he went.*

**pull** | pŏol | —*verb* **pulled, pulling** To draw something toward oneself: *In a game of tug of war, you must pull on the rope as hard as you can.*

**pur•sue** | pər **soō**′ | —*verb* **pursued, pursuing 1.** To chase or follow in order to catch: *The cat pursued the mouse.* **2.** To keep trying to reach: *I will pursue my goal to be a doctor.*

**put** | pŏot | —*verb* **put, putting** To place; to set: *Allen put the cookies in the cookie jar.*

# Q

**quart** | kwôrt | —*noun, plural* **quarts**
**1.** Unit of measure equal to two pints or one quarter of a gallon: *I was so thirsty, I drank a quart of juice.* **2.** Container that holds a quart: *Jerry bought a quart of milk.*

**queen** | kwēn | —*noun, plural* **queens**
**1.** A woman who rules over a country: *Queen Elizabeth is the ruler of England.* **2.** The wife of a king: *The king and the queen lived in a castle.*

**qui•et** | **kwī**′ it | —*adjective* **quieter, quietest** Silent; making little or no sound: *Laura was quiet so that she wouldn't wake her baby brother.*

# R

**rain** | rān | —*noun* Drops of water that fall from the clouds: *The rain washed away Jan's sand castle.* —*verb* **rained, raining** To fall in drops of water from the clouds: *Ann didn't have to water the grass because it had rained all night.*

**read** | rēd | —*verb* **read** | rĕd |, **reading** To look at and get the meaning of something written or printed: *Every day I read the comics in the newspaper. I've already read the comics today.*

**read•y** | **rĕd**′ ē | —*adjective* **readier, readiest** Prepared to do something: *Doris was packed and ready to go.*

**re•joice** | rĭ **jois′** | —*verb* **rejoiced, rejoicing** To show or feel great joy: *We rejoice when our team wins.*

**right** | rīt | —*adjective* **1.** Opposite the left side: *I throw a ball with my right arm.* **2.** Correct; true; just: *Telling the truth is the right thing to do.* —*adverb* Straight on; directly: *I turned around without looking and walked right into a wall.* • **Right** sounds like **write.**

**riv•er** | rĭv′ ər | —*noun, plural* **rivers** A large stream of water that flows into a lake, ocean, sea, or another river: *My dad and I go fishing in the river.*

**road** | rōd | —*noun, plural* **roads** An open way for travel between two or more places: *Do you remember how Dorothy followed the yellow brick road to Oz?*

**ro•dent** | rōd′ nt | —*noun, plural* **rodents** Any of a large group of animals such as mice, rats, squirrels, or beavers that have large front teeth used for gnawing: *We try to keep rodents out of the house.*

**ro•de•o** | rō′ dē ō′ | or | ro dā′ o | —*noun, plural* **rodeos** A show where people show their skill in contests such as riding horses and roping cattle: *It is fun to go to a rodeo.*

**roy•al** | roi′ əl | —*adjective* **1.** Of or having to do with kings or queens: *The prince was a member of the royal family.* **2.** Fit for a king or queen; splendid: *The queen lived in a royal palace.*

# S

**safe** | sāf | —*adjective* **safer, safest** Free from danger or harm: *Police officers help make the streets safe.*

**said** | sĕd | Look up **say.**

**sail** | sāl | —*noun, plural* **sails** A piece of strong material spread to catch the wind and make a boat move: *As the wind filled the sails, the sailboat*

moved faster. —*verb* **sailed, sailing** **1.** To travel across the water on a ship: *The ship is going to sail across the ocean to Europe.* **2.** To steer a boat: *I sailed the boat across the lake all by myself.*

**Sat•ur•day** | săt′ ər dē | or | săt′ ər dā′ | —*noun, plural* **Saturdays** The seventh day of the week: *Mom took us to the baseball game on Saturday.*

**sau•sage** | sô′ sĭj | —*noun, plural* **sausages** Chopped meat that is mixed with spices and stuffed into a thin tube-shaped casing: *We had sausage for breakfast.*

**save** | sāv | —*verb* **saved, saving 1.** To free from danger or harm: *Marie saved Ellen from falling off the swing.* **2.** To avoid wasting: *I took the bus instead of walking to save time.*

**say** | sā | —*verb* **says** | sĕz | , **said** | sĕd | , **saying** To speak; to talk: *Grandma says it's time for dinner.*

**scheme** | skēm | —*noun, plural* **schemes** A plan or plot for doing something: *Mark has a scheme for doing his homework.*

**school¹** | skōol | —*noun, plural* **schools** A place of teaching and learning: *We learned about Japan in school.*

**school²** | skōol | —*noun, plural* **schools** A large group of fish that swim together: *While we were fishing, a school of guppies swam by.*

**sea** | sē | —*noun, plural* **seas** The great body of water that covers about three-fourths of the earth's surface; ocean: *Whales live in the sea.*

215

**seam** | sēm | —*noun, plural* **seams** A line or fold formed by sewing together two pieces of cloth or other material: *The seam on the shirt ripped.*

**sec•ond**[1] | sĕk′ ənd | —*noun, plural* **seconds** A unit of time equal to 1/60 of one minute: *Janet finished the test in 3 minutes and 10 seconds flat.*

**sec•ond**[2] | sĕk′ ənd | —*adjective* Next after the first: *Mike came in first in the race, and I came in second.*

**send** | sĕnd | —*verb* **sent** | sĕnt | , **sending** To cause or order to go: *Dad sent me to the store to buy ice cream for dessert.*

**sent** | sĕnt | Look up **send.** • **Sent** sounds like **cent.**

**Sep•tem•ber** | sĕp tĕm′ bər | —*noun* The ninth month of the year. September has 30 days: *In September we go back to school.*

**shake** | shāk | —*verb* **shook** | sho͝ok | , **shaken, shaking 1.** To tremble or quiver: *I was so scared, my whole body began to shake.* **2.** To cause to move: *The boys shook the tree, and all the leaves fell off.*

**shak•y** | shā′ kē | —*adjective* **shakier, shakiest 1.** Trembling; shaking: *Her voice was shakier than mine.* **2.** Not firm; likely to break down: *Kevin's bike is the shakiest I have ever ridden.*

**sharp** | shärp | —*adjective* **sharper, sharpest 1.** Something having a thin, cutting edge or point: *Anna needed a sharper knife to cut her tough steak.* **2.** Quickly aware of things; keen: *Owls' sharp eyesight helps them to see in the dark.*

**she'll** | shēl | The contraction of "she will": *My mother says she'll pick us up after practice.*

**she's** | shēz | The contraction of "she is" or "she has": *Molly says she's going to swim across the lake, but she's never done it before.*

**shine** | shīn | —*verb* **shone** | shōn | or **shined, shining 1.** To give off or reflect light: *Stop shining the flashlight at me.* **2.** To polish: *I polished my shoes until they shone.*

**shook** | sho͝ok | Look up **shake.**

**shop** | shŏp | —*noun, plural* **shops** A store; a place where goods are sold: *Don's favorite shop is Happy Toy Store.* —*verb* **shopped, shopping** To visit stores to buy things: *My brother and I went shopping for a pet frog.*

**should** | sho͝od | —*helping* or *auxiliary verb* Ought to; have a duty to: *I should practice the piano every day.*

**shove** | shŭv | —*verb* **shoved, shoving** To push roughly: *When Mom came into my room, I shoved the present under the bed.* —*noun, plural* **shoves** A push: *My dog wouldn't move so I gave him a little shove.*

**show** | shō | —*verb* **showed, showed** or **shown, showing 1.** To make known; to reveal: *It shows on my face when I'm sad.* **2.** To place in sight: *Let's show everyone our bowling trophy.* —*noun, plural* **shows** Any kind of public performance, entertainment, or display: *Ms. Cook's class put on an art show at school.*

**shrewd** | shro͞od | —*adjective* **shrewder, shrewdest** Clever and smart: *The shrewd buyer looked for the best price.*

**size** | sīz | —*noun, plural* **sizes** The height, width, or length of a thing: *The twins, Billy and Barry, have always been the same size.*

**sketch** | skĕch | —*noun, plural* **sketches** A rough quick drawing or outline:

*The sketch of the tree was pretty good.* —verb **sketched, sketching** To make a sketch: *The artist sketched the child's face.*

**sky** | skī | —noun, plural **skies** The air high above the earth; the heavens: *I fly my kite high up in the sky.*

**sky•line** | skī′ līn′ | —noun, plural **skylines** 1. The outline of buildings or other objects as seen against the sky: *We could see the city's skyline from the airplane.* 2. The line at which the earth and sky seem to meet.

**sleep** | slēp | —noun A natural rest of body and mind; state of not being awake: *I'm so tired, I could use a week of sleep.* —verb **slept, sleeping** To be in or to fall into a state of sleep: *The bear slept in his den all winter.*

**sleep•y** | slē′ pē | —adjective **sleepier, sleepiest** Ready for sleep; drowsy: *When I am sleepy, I start to yawn.*

**slow** | slō | —adverb **slower, slowest** Not quick: *Bobby walks slower than a turtle.* —verb **slowed, slowing** To cause to move slow or slower: *I stepped on the brakes to slow down my bike.*

**slump** | slŭmp | —verb **slumped, slumping** To fall or sink down suddenly: *Mother told me not to slump at the dinner table.*

**smudge** | smŭj | —noun, plural **smudges** A dirty mark or smear: *Betsy had a smudge on the birthday card.* —verb **smudged, smudging** To make dirty or smeared.

**sneeze** | snēz | —verb **sneezed, sneezing** To force air to pass suddenly with force from the nose and mouth. A tickling inside the nose causes a person to sneeze: *When John caught a cold, he sneezed for two days.*

**snow** | snō | —noun, plural **snows** Soft white flakes of frozen water vapor that form in the sky and fall to the earth: *Jeremy loved to ride his sled in the snow.* —verb **snowed, snowing** To fall as snow: *When it stopped snowing, I had to shovel the walk.*

**sock** | sŏk | —noun, plural **socks** A short stocking reaching no higher than the knee: *I stepped in a puddle and got my shoes and socks soaked.*

**sog•gy** | sô′ gē | —adjective **soggier, soggiest** Very wet; soaked: *My shoes were soggy after I played in the rain.*

**soil**[1] | soil | —noun, plural **soils** The loose top layer of the earth's surface in which plants grow: *My class planted a little tree in the soil.*

**soil**[2] | soil | —verb **soiled, soiling** To make dirty: *Jane soiled her clean shirt.*

**so•lo** | sō′ lō | —adjective Done by one person alone: *The pilot made her first solo flight.* —noun, plural **solos** Music that one person plays or sings all alone.

**some** | sŭm | —adjective A few; a little: *Some people like pizza, and some people don't.* • **Some** sounds like **sum.**

**some•bod•y** | sŭm′ bŏd′ ē | —pronoun A person not known or named: *Somebody lost a hat.*

**some•thing** | sŭm′ thĭng | —pronoun A particular thing that is not named or known: *I want something to eat, but I don't know what.*

**sor•ry** | sŏr′ ē | or | sôr′ ē | — adjective **sorrier, sorriest** Feeling sadness, regret, or pity: *Suzy was sorry that she lost her sister's record.*

**sound** | sound | —noun, plural **sounds** Something that is heard; sensation made by vibrations in the air and picked up by the ear: *We were surprised to hear thumping sounds coming from the empty attic.*

**spend** | spĕnd | —verb **spent** | spĕnt | , **spending** 1. To pay out money: *He spent a lot of money for a new bat.* 2. To pass time: *Katy spent the whole day at the carnival.*

**spent** | spĕnt | Look up **spend.**

**spin·ach** | **spĭn′** ĭch | —*noun* A plant with dark green leaves that is eaten as a vegetable: *We had spinach for dinner.*

**spoil** | spoil | —*verb* **spoiled** or **spoilt, spoiling 1.** To ruin or damage: *The rain spoiled the class picnic.* **2.** To become unfit for use: *The milk will spoil if you forget to keep it cold.*

**sport** | spôrt | or | spōrt | —*noun, plural* **sports** A game or contest requiring physical activity: *My favorite sport is soccer.*

**spring** | sprĭng | —*noun, plural* **springs 1.** The season between winter and summer: *In the spring the flowers start to bloom.* **2.** A place where water flows to the surface of the ground: *A fish swam near the spring.*

**stair** | stâr | —*noun, plural* **stairs** A step in a flight of steps: *Tommy climbed the stairs to his room.*

**star** | stär | —*noun, plural* **stars 1.** Any heavenly body, other than the moon or planets, seen from Earth in the night sky: *The best part of camping is watching the stars at night.* **2.** A famous person in any field or profession: *Who is your favorite movie star?*

**starch** | stärch | —*noun, plural* **starches 1.** White food matter that is made and stored in parts of plants: *Corn has starch in it.* **2.** A product that is used to make cloth stiff: *Ken put starch in the shirt.*

**start** | stärt | —*verb* **started, starting** To begin to go somewhere or do something: *Let's start a fan club.*

**stood** | sto͝od | Look up **stand.**

**stop** | stŏp | —*verb* **stopped, stopping** To cease; to come to a halt: *When the rain stopped, Steven went out to play.*

**storm** | stôrm | —*noun, plural* **storms** Strong winds accompanied by rain, hail, sand, or snow: *The storm blew down a big tree.*

**sto·ry** | **stôr′** ē | or | **stōr′** ē | —*noun, plural* **stories 1.** An account of something that has happened: *Did you read the story?* **2.** A tale of fiction: *Phil tells his sister a bedtime story before she goes to sleep.*

**street** | strēt | —*noun, plural* **streets** A road in a city or town that is usually lined with buildings: *My house is on the same street as yours.*

**strong** | strông | or | strŏng | —*adjective* **stronger, strongest** Having much power or strength: *John Henry was strong enough to beat the steam drill.*

**stun** | stŭn | —*verb* **stunned, stunning 1.** To daze or make unconscious: *Jack was stunned when he bumped his head.* **2.** To shock: *Tom was stunned by the news.*

**sub·tract** | səb **trăkt′** | —*verb* **subtracted, subtracting** To take away: *Subtract two cents from eight cents, and you'll have six cents.*

**such** | sŭch | —*adjective* Of this kind or that kind: *I didn't know you would wear such shoes.* —*adverb* Especially: *That was such a nice party.*

**sum** | sŭm | —*noun, plural* **sums** The number you get when you add two or more numbers: *The sum of 5 cookies and 6 cookies is 11 cookies.* • **Sum** sounds like **some.**

**sum·mer** | **sŭm′** ər | —*noun, plural* **summers** The warmest season of the year. Summer comes between spring and fall: *Tim goes to camp every summer.*

**sun** | sŭn | —*noun* The star around which the Earth and other planets revolve. The sun is the source of light and heat: *I wake up when the sun rises in the morning.* • **Sun** sounds like **son.**

**Sun•day** | **sŭn**′ dē | or | **sŭn**′ dā′ | —*noun, plural* **Sundays** The first day of the week: *On Sunday Inga went to church.*

**sun•ny** | **sŭn**′ ē | —*adjective* Having much sun: *It was a sunny day at the beach.*

**sup•per** | **sŭp**′ ər | —*noun, plural* **suppers** The evening meal or the last meal of the day: *My family ate supper at a restaurant last night.*

**sure** | shŏŏr | —*adjective* **surer, surest** Feeling certain; having no doubt: *Are you sure you don't want a piece of cake?*

**sur•geon** | **sûr**′ jən | —*noun, plural* **surgeons** A doctor who performs surgery: *The surgeon operated on my foot.*

## T

**ta•ble** | **tā**′ bəl | —*noun, plural* **tables** A piece of furniture having a flat top supported by legs: *Dinner was already on the table when I got home.*

**take** | tāk | —*verb* **took** | tŏŏk | , **taken, taking** **1.** To get; accept: *Mike took the award for the whole team.* **2.** To carry to a different place: *I am taking your suitcase upstairs.* **3.** To move; remove: *Claire took her watch off her hand.*

**talk** | tôk | —*verb* **talked, talking** To speak; utter words: *We were talking about Mark, when he walked in.* —*noun* **1.** An informal speech: *I gave a talk in science class.* **2.** A rumor; gossip: *There was talk that school would be closed tomorrow because of the snow.*

**tall** | tôl | —*adjective* **taller, tallest** **1.** Of more than average height: *Ben is five inches taller than I am.* **2.** Hard to believe; exaggerated: *Who would believe that tall story?*

**team** | tēm | —*noun, plural* **teams** **1.** Two or more animals harnessed together to work: *Granddad used to plow the field with a team of horses.* **2.** A group of people playing on the same side in a game: *The whole school came to watch our baseball team win.*

**teen•ag•er** | **tēn**′ ā′ jər | —*noun, plural* **teenagers** A person who is between the ages of thirteen and nineteen: *My older sister is a teenager.*

**tell** | tĕl | —*verb* **told** | tōld | , **telling** To put into words; to say: *I told Dad what had happened at school today.*

**test** | tĕst | —*noun, plural* **tests** **1.** A series of questions that judge a person's skill or knowledge: *I studied hard to pass my spelling test.* **2.** A way to find out the quality of something: *Lifting weights will test how strong you are.* —*verb* **tested, testing** To put to a test; to try out: *I tested the yo-yo to make sure it worked before I bought it.*

**thank** | thăngk | —*verb* **thanked, thanking** To say that one is grateful or pleased: *The boys and girls thanked the magician for the show.*

**them** | thĕm | —*pronoun* Persons, things, or animals spoken or written about: *After Connie made the peanut butter cookies, she put them in the cookie jar.*

**then** | thĕn | —*adverb* **1.** At the time: *I used to sleep with a teddy bear, but I was only a kid then.* **2.** After that: *We saw lightning flash and then we heard the thunder roar.* **3.** A time mentioned: *Go finish your homework and by then dinner will be ready.*

**there'd** | thârd | The contraction for "there would": *There'd be ten people at the party if they all come.*

**there'll** | thârl | The contraction for "there will": *There'll be a baseball game tomorrow.*

**these** | thēz | Look up **this.**

219

**they** | *thā* | —*pronoun* **1.** The people, animals, or things named before: *Mr. Martin gave us six arithmetic problems, and they were all hard.* **2.** People in general: *They used to think the world was flat.*

**they'd** | *thā*d | The contraction of "they had" or "they would": *I asked Don and Bill if they'd seen my cat anywhere. Don and Bill said they'd treat me to an ice cream cone.*

**they'll** | *thā*l | The contraction of "they will" or "they shall": *Arnold and Bonnie said they'll bring the cake to the party.*

**they've** | *thā*v | The contraction of "they have": *The twins say they've never gone fishing.*

**thing** | *thĭng* | —*noun, plural* **things** **1.** Any object or substance that cannot be named exactly: *What is that green thing on the floor?* **2.** An act; a deed: *Hitting that home run was the best thing I ever did.*

**think** | *thĭngk* | —*verb* **thought, thinking** **1.** To use the mind to come to an opinion: *I think I should go home now.* **2.** To have in mind: *Julia thinks she would like to be a doctor.*

**third** | *thûrd* | —*noun, plural* **thirds** One of three equal parts: *Roger ate a third of the pizza.* —*adjective* Next after second: *Alice was the third person in line for the concert.*

**this** | *thĭs* | —*adjective, plural* **these** | *thēz* | Referring to a thing or person nearby or just mentioned: *Move these toys before you trip over them.* —*pronoun, plural* **these** A thing or person nearby or just mentioned: *This is our secret clubhouse.*

**Thurs·day** | **thûrz**′ dē | or | **thûrz**′ dā′ | —*noun, plural* **Thursdays** The fifth day of the week: *Art class meets every Thursday after school.*

**times** | *tīmz* | —*preposition* Multiplied by: *Three times two equals six.*

**ti·ny** | **tī**′ nē | —*adjective* **tinier, tiniest** Very small: *The kitten was so tiny, it fit in my hand.*

**tire¹** | *tīr* | —*verb* **tired, tiring** To become weary: *Lee tired after hiking all day.*

**tire²** | *tīr* | —*noun, plural* **tires** A band of rubber around the rim of a wheel: *My bicycle has a flat tire.*

**toast** | *tōst* | —*verb* **toasted, toasting** To brown by heating: *We toasted marshmallows over the campfire.* —*noun* A slice of bread heated and browned on both sides: *I always have toast with my breakfast.*

**toe** | *tō* | —*noun, plural* **toes** One of the five separate divisions of the foot: *Ellen put her big toe into the bath water to see if it was too hot.*

**too** | *tōō* | —*adverb* **1.** Also; besides: *Adam had to make the salad and set the table, too.* **2.** Very: *This soup is too hot to eat.* • **Too** sounds like **two.**

**took** | *tŏŏk* | Look up **take.**

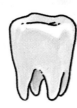

**tooth** | *tōōth* | —*noun, plural* **teeth** Any of the hard, white, bony parts in the mouth used for biting and chewing: *Judy's front tooth is ready to fall out.*

**tow·er** | **tou**′ ər | —*noun, plural* **towers** A high structure or a part of a building rising higher than the rest of it: *Rapunzel was hidden away in a tower so that no one could reach her.*

**town** | *toun* | —*noun, plural* **towns** A group of houses or buildings that is larger than a village but smaller than a city: *My aunt is the new mayor of our town.*

**toy** | *toi* | —*noun, plural* **toys** Something a child plays with: *Johnny's favorite toy is Robbie-the-Robot.*

**train** | *trān* | —*noun, plural* **trains** Connected railroad cars pulled by an engine or powered by electricity:

*Mom and I went by train to visit Aunt Bess.*

**true** | trōō | —*adjective* **truer, truest** Not false; according to fact: *Only June knows the true story.*

**try** | trī | —*verb* **tried, trying, tries** To make an effort; to attempt: *Will you try to cheer up Debbie?*

**Tues•day** | tōōz′ dē | *or* | tōōz′ dā′ | *or* | tyōōz′ dē | *or* | tyōōz′ dā′ | —*noun, plural* **Tuesdays** The third day of the week: *I go to the library every Tuesday.*

**turn** | tûrn | —*verb* **turned, turning** 1. To move round; rotate: *The Earth turns on its axis once every 24 hours.* 2. To change direction or position: *The path turned into the woods.* —*noun, plural* **turns** A chance to do something after someone else: *Finally, it was Jenny's turn at bat.*

**two** | tōō | —*noun* One more than one: *The twins are two of my good buddies.* • **Two** sounds like **too.**

# U

**un•der** | ŭn′ dər | —*preposition* 1. Below; beneath: *I put my shoes under my bed.* 2. Less than: *Sue was under 12, so she went to the movies for half-price.*

**use** | yōōz | —*verb* **used, using** To put into service: *I used the whole day to finish my science project.*
   ***Idiom.* used to.** Familiar with: *I was used to sleeping with the light on.*

**used** | yōōzd | —*adjective* Not new: *Nick bought a used bike.*

# V

**va•ri•e•ty** | və rī′ ĭ tē | —*noun, plural* **varieties** 1. A different kind within the same group: *We had a new variety of soup for lunch.* 2. Change

or difference: *I like variety in my day.*

**ver•y** | vĕr′ ē | —*adverb* Much; extremely: *That joke was very funny.*

**voice** | vois | —*noun, plural* **voices** The sound coming from the mouth: *Bernice has a wonderful voice.*

# W

**waf•fle** | wŏf′ əl | —*noun, plural* **waffles** A crisp cake made of batter: *Dad made waffles for breakfast.*

**wait** | wāt | —*verb* **waited, waiting** To stay until someone comes or something happens: *We could hardly wait for the cartoon to start.* • **Wait** sounds like **weight.**

**walk** | wôk | —*verb* **walked, walking** To go on foot at a steady pace: *The elephant walked slowly around the big circus tent.*

**was** | wŏz | or | wŭz | or | wəz | Look up **be.**

**wash** | wŏsh | or | wôsh | —*verb,* **washed, washing** To clean with a liquid, usually water: *I'll wash if you dry.*

**was•n't** | wŏz ənt | or | wŭz ənt | The contraction of "was not": *Bill wasn't ready when his friends arrived.*

**wa•ter** | wô′ tər | or | wŏt′ ər | —*noun* 1. The colorless, tasteless, odorless liquid that fills oceans, rivers, and ponds: *Water falls from the sky as rain.* 2. A lake, river, pool, or any other body of this liquid: *We went for a swim in the water.* —*verb* **watered, watering** To sprinkle or provide with water: *The rain watered the grass for me.*

**we'd** | wēd | The contraction of "we had," "we should," or "we would": *We'd better call our parents before we walk home. We'd sing a song, but we cannot find the music.*

**Wed•nes•day** | wĕnz′ dē | or | wĕnz′ dā′ | —*noun, plural* **Wednesdays** The fourth day of the week: *We have cooking class on Wednesday.*

**weigh** | wā | —*verb,* **weighed, weighing**
**1.** To find out how heavy something is by using a scale: *Mom lets me weigh the vegetables before she buys them.* **2.** To have a certain weight: *Jason's dog, Mimi, weighs only 11 pounds.*

**weird** | wîrd | —*adjective* **weirder, weirdest 1.** Causing an uneasy feeling; mysterious: *A weirder noise came from the cave today than yesterday.* **2.** Strange; odd; unusual: *That is the weirdest story I have ever read.*

**we'll** | wēl | The contraction of "we will" or "we shall": *We'll go into the Fun House with you.*

**were** | wûr | Look up **be.**

**were•n't** | wûrnt | or | **wûr′** ənt | The contraction of "were not": *My friends weren't home when I stopped by.*

**we've** | wēv | The contraction of "we have": *We've still got a lot of work to do on the tree house.*

**wharf** | wôrf | —*noun, plural* **wharves** A landing place for boats and ships built along a shore; dock: *Five boats were next to the wharf.*

**what** | hwŏt | or | hwŭt | or | wŏt | or | wŭt | or | hwət | or | wət | —*pronoun*
**1.** Which thing or things: *What do you want me to do?* **2.** The thing which: *She didn't know what her mother would say about her report card.* **3.** Which: *What color do you want to paint your room?*

**wheel** | hwēl | or | wēl | —*noun, plural* **wheels** A round frame supported by spokes on which a vehicle moves:

*Have you ever been on the Ferris wheel?*

**when** | hwĕn | or | wĕn | —*adverb* **1.** At what time: *When will you be ready to go?* **2.** At a particular time: *I'll call you when I get to Aunt Sara's house.*

**where** | hwâr | or | wâr | —*adverb* **1.** At what place: *Where are my mittens?* **2.** To what place: *Where are we going on our class trip?*

**where'd** | hwârd | or | wârd | The contraction of "where did": *Where'd you leave your coat?*

**which** | hwĭch | or | wĭch | —*pronoun*
**1.** Which one or ones: *Which is my ice cream cone?* **2.** That: *I bought my mother a present, which I know she will like.* —*adjective* What one or ones: *Pam couldn't tell which cowboy hat was hers.*

**while** | hwīl | or | wīl | —*noun* A period of time: *Please stay for a while.* —*conjunction* **1.** At the same time that: *Mom read the newspaper while I did my homework.* **2.** Although: *Ron was short while his brothers were tall.*

**white** | hwīt | or | wīt | —*noun* The lightest color; the color of snow: *White is the color of the clouds on a sunny day.* —*adjective* **whiter, whitest** Having the color white: *I have white shoes.*

**who** | hoo | —*pronoun* What person or persons: *Who is your best friend?*

**whole** | hōl | —*adjective* **1.** Not broken; complete: *Is this a whole deck of cards?* **2.** Entire amount: *I ate the whole pie by myself.* • **Whole** sounds like **hole.**

**who'll** | hool | The contraction of "who will" or "who shall": *Who'll bring the games?*

**why** | hwī | or | wī | —*adverb* For what reason: *Why is your tongue green?*

**width** | wĭdth | —*noun, plural* **widths** The distance from side to side: *The width of the room is ten feet.*

**wild•flow•er** | wīld′ flou′ ər | —*noun, plural* **wildflowers** Flowers on a wild plant: *The wildflowers were pretty.*

**will** | wĭl | —*helping* or *auxiliary verb* Intention: *I will go to the picnic.*

**win** | wĭn | —*verb,* **won** | wŭn |, **winning** To gain a victory: *Who won the Ping-Pong contest?*

**win•ter** | wĭn′ tər | —*noun, plural* **winters** The coldest season of the year, coming between fall and spring: *I don't like to shovel snow in the winter.*

**wire** | wīr | —*noun, plural* **wires** Metal drawn out into a thin thread: *The fence around the farm was made of wire.*

**wish** | wĭsh | —*noun, plural* **wishes** A strong desire: *Renee's only wish was to be finished with her work.* —*verb* **wished, wishing** To have a desire for something: *Ken wished he could meet his favorite singing star.*

**won** | wŭn | Look up **win.**

**won't** | wōnt | The contraction of "will not": *I won't be at the park today.*

**wood** | wŏod | —*noun* The hard material making up the trunk and branches of a tree: *The cabin was built of wood.* • **Wood** sounds like **would.**

**word** | wûrd | —*noun, plural* **words** A sound or group of sounds having a certain meaning: *I missed only one word on my spelling test.*

**work** | wûrk | —*noun* **1.** The effort made in doing or making something: *Mowing the lawn is hard work.* **2.** A task: *I can't go because I have too much school work to do.* —*verb* **worked, working** To have a job: *Joe worked at the supermarket after school.*

**world** | wûrld | —*noun* The Earth: *In history class we learn about the world.*

**worm** | wûrm | —*noun, plural* **worms** A crawling creature with a long, slender body: *There are lots of worms in the backyard.*

**would** | wŏod | —*helping* or *auxiliary verb* Past tense of **will,** meaning was or were intending to: *I knew you would come sooner or later.* • **Would** sounds like **wood.**

**would•n't** | wŏod′ nt | The contraction of "would not": *Sam knew he wouldn't get home on time unless he ran.*

**would•'ve** | wŏod′ əv | The contraction of "would have": *Josh would've cleaned his room, but he was late for school.*

**write** | rīt | —*verb* **wrote** | rōt |, **written, writing** To make letters or words with a pen, pencil, etc.: *Karen promised to write to me when she went on vacation. I wrote to my sister from my aunt's.*

**wrote** | rōt | Look up **write.**

# Y

**yard¹** | yärd | —*noun, plural* **yards** A unit of length measuring 3 feet or 36 inches: *This room is three yards long.*

**yard²** | yärd | —*noun, plural* **yards** A piece of land near a building: *My house has a big yard to play in.*

**year** | yîr | —*noun, plural* **years** The length of time it takes the Earth to go around the sun once; 365 days: *This year I will be 10 years old.*

**yel•low** | yĕl′ ō | —*noun* The color of gold or butter: *Yellow is the color of ripe lemons.* —*adjective* **yellower, yellowest** Having this color: *I wore my yellow shirt with my blue pants.*

**you'd** | yŏod | The contraction of "you had" or "you would": *You'd better go to bed before you fall asleep in the chair. I know that you'd really like to join our club.*

**you'll** | yŏol | The contraction of "you will" or "you shall": *You broke this vase, so you'll have to pay for it.*

**you've** | yŏov | The contraction of "you have": *You've got a turtle just like mine.*

# THE CHECKPOINT
# Study Plan

When you have finished a Checkpoint page and you know that you have the correct answers, use the Checkpoint page and this Study Plan to test yourself.

★ Cover your answers to the Checkpoint page with a piece of paper. Number the paper 1 through 16. For each spelling clue, do steps 1, 2, and 3.

**1** Read the clue and say the answer.

**2** Spell the answer aloud.

**3** Write the answer

★ Uncover your first answers and do steps 4, 5, and 6.

**4** Check your answers.

**5** Circle the number of each misspelled word.

**6** Write the correct spelling next to each incorrect word.

★ To study, cover your answers again, and fold the paper so that only the numbers show. For each circled number, repeat steps 1 through 6.